THE CONTEXT EATING METHOD FOR WOMEN

How to Lose Weight Without Sucking all the Gluten, Chocolate and Wine-Filled Joy from your Life

Meal plan and recipes included

Darpan Ahluwalia and Kathy Ryan

Registered Holistic Nutritionists

THE CONTEXT EATING METHOD FOR WOMEN

HOW TO LOSE WEIGHT WITHOUT SUCKING ALL THE GLUTEN, CHOCOLATE AND WINE-FILLED JOY FROM YOUR LIFE

DARPAN ALHUWALIA AND KATHY RYAN

LUCKY BOOK PUBLISHING

FREE GIFT!

As a reader of this book, you can get the book resources (Triggered Eating Inventory, Meal Plans, and Recipes) for free at:

www.luckybookpublishing.com/contexteating

OR scan the QR code below!

CONTENTS

DISCLAIMER

Results may vary. The information presented in this work is by no way intended as medical advice or as a substitute for medical counseling. The information should be used in conjunction with the guidance and care of your physician. Consult your physician before beginning any health or weight loss program. If you choose not to obtain the consent of your physician and/or work with your physician while making use of the suggestions in this book and other resources, you are agreeing to accept full responsibility for your outcomes.

We dedicate this book to our amazing families, friends, and clients.

Darpan To my three kids. You are my world, and I give thanks for you every day. To the fierce tribe of women who have stood with me through thick and thin. You know who you are, and together we are creating a legacy. To my parents and siblings for your unconditional love and support.

Kathy To my amazing kiddo and her baby boy. We've been through it and are still standing. LUM. To my friends and mentors who helped shape my ideas and words, hugged me, and exhorted me so that I never settled. To my family, who have watched and supported and loved me through it all.

To our clients who have trusted us and who we have learned from over the decades. Thank you for your vulnerability, your honesty and your continued support. You are why we do what we do.

To Samantha and Simar, our amazing publishing team duo. Thank you for helping us bring our little project to life and out to the world!

- Darpan and Kathy

INTRODUCTION

It is 9:08 p.m. on a Sunday. I am ready for my "I'll Start Monday" #1345 to begin in less than eight hours. I will be up at 5 a.m. to start my workout. I have sworn off chocolate and sugar forever. I will finally drink three liters of water to make my liver happy, and my skin glow. The path to my beautifully toned body and my entrance into the exclusive self-disciplined-yoga-mat- carrying-perfectly-manicured-mommy-club is only eight weeks away.

This is the Monday that will count as the day my life changed forever. I know this day will be different from all the previous "I'll Start Mondays" (ISMs) I have committed to over the years. I am motivated and ready to go.

5:00 a.m. Monday. I am rudely awakened from my sound sleep as my jarring alarm goes off. I jump out of bed, half asleep but enthusiastic, visualizing my soon-to-be health and stunning beauty. I run downstairs and quickly remove the laundry drying on the treadmill and create some space among the boxes to do some stretching.

But, within seconds of tying my first shoe, the voices in my head begin their barrage.

First, they affirm all the good reasons why being awake at 5 a.m. to work out is not necessary:

"You need more sleep!"

"You're going to burn out."

"There are millions of people in worse shape than you."

"You're a busy mom. People understand you're too busy to work out."

"You're going to be exhausted by 3 p.m."

"The sun is not even up yet."

"I think you may be getting a cold – you'd better rest."

"You're going to wake the kids."

I manage to ignore them and begin my pre-planned routine. They come back for round two and start to play on my insecurities:

"You're not an athlete."

Look at you trying to do that Yoga pose – pathetic."

"You'll never lose the flab on your arms."

"Helllllo muffin top – yikes."

"Um, if you're going to be running on a treadmill, you need to invest in a better sports bra."

I struggle pathetically through 18.23 mins of awkward stretching, arm weights, and 56 seconds of running before the voices in round three start breaking through.

"That's enough for today; you don't want to overdo it."

"One hour? You'll never make it, not a chance."

"You don't want to be sore."

"You really need to get better music/shoes/bra, etc."

"Hey, didn't you forget to make lunches/send the email/fold the laundry/clean the bathroom?"

"You have to pee."

Yes, I really do have to pee.

Twenty-two minutes into my "I'll Start Monday" #1345, I am ready to postpone my health goals and return to the comfort of my bed. I feel awkward, pathetic, unsure of what I am supposed to be doing, and suddenly very unmotivated.

"WHAT-IS-WRONG-WITH-YOU!?" (Round four begins).

The voices are never satisfied. Never happy. Impossible to please.

I answer that terrible question with everything my current perspective tells me is true.

I am pathetic, lazy, undisciplined, delusional, fat, ugly, tired, unmotivated, selfish, weak, unorganized, clumsy, awkward, and in desperate need of some serious kegel exercises, an extra large coffee with triple sugar, and some chocolate for breakfast.

That's what's wrong with me. At this moment, this is who I am. This is what I feel, and this is how I react.

Have you been there?

Have you ever bought and made a week's worth of healthy food and then ordered take-out on the way home from work?

Have you ever vowed "never to eat sugar again" and go to the store later that same day and buy a pint of Ben and Jerry's (because it was on sale), and you don't even usually eat ice cream?

Have you ever thought that eating carrots or grapes would curb your craving for that chocolate-covered-whatever that you "hid from yourself" in the freezer?

Have you ever bought a twelve-month gym membership and used it three times (twice in January and once in September?)

Are the voices in your head constantly asking bad questions like, "WHAT IS WRONG WITH YOU?!" and do they demand an answer?

The thing about "I'll Start Mondays" is that they are always preceded by "Just-One-More" Fun-Day-Sunday.

Just one more day, just one more brownie, just one more bag of chips, just one more glass of wine, just one more piece of pizza, just one more day of binge-watching Netflix, just one more day of not going to the gym. Essentially you have just one more day of doing all the things you love, eating all the things you love eating, and avoiding all the things you don't enjoy.

Then, at the stroke of midnight, you will suddenly turn into this brand-new person, flip your life entirely on its head and start avoiding all the things you love doing and eating and start engaging in all the things you don't really enjoy at all.

Whelp, when you put it that way, that's completely insane.

There must be a better way….?

How do you eliminate "I'll Start Mondays" from your life and silence the unsupportive, destructive voices in your head? How do you get where you need to go with your health without sucking all the glutinous, chocolate, and wine-filled joy from your life? How do you motivate yourself to move forward in the direction you need to go without having to play the "all or nothing game"?

That, my friend, is precisely what this book is all about because, quite frankly, I am tired.

I am tired of women assessing their value based on the size of their jeans or the shape of their curves.

I am done with the idea that there is a narrow definition for what defines a "bikini body."

I am no longer supportive of restrictive eating and all-or-nothing approaches that lead women to binge or engage in other forms of disordered eating.

I am finished with numbers, counting, scales, and most women gaining back the weight they lost within two years.

I am calling out women who say things like "I was bad today" because they had a piece of cake at their son's birthday party.

I am railing against the idea that women over forty need to look like they are in their twenties when they are also taught to put themselves last behind their kids, partners, career, and clients.

I am done listening to the "experts" and their restrictive approaches that FORCE the body to lose pounds through precise math calculations and nutrient intake because once the precise approach is no longer followed, the yo-yo begins again!

I am tired, and I am ready to ditch "I'll Start Mondays" and "New Year New You" and the dieting trap for good.

I am ready for an alternative to dieting that teaches me how to keep my weight at a healthier level but does not become the all-encompassing focus of my life or the one thing that determines my value or happiness.

I am ready for something that acknowledges that I don't aspire to fit into the jeans that I wore in high school or get down to 15% body fat, but that also keeps my weight from climbing to levels that impede my health and quality of life.

I am ready to embrace the beneficial aspects of the body positivity and intuitive eating movements while also understanding that I need some healthy eating parameters so that I don't slowly kill myself with food.

Are you with me?

It's time to stop dieting and start context eating.

CHAPTER 1

WHAT IS CONTEXT EATING?

Context Eating is an alternative to dieting.

Diet culture is limited in its focus because its sole objective is to control WHAT you eat. This is a narrow approach to weight loss and health in general and is the most significant factor influencing why so many people cannot stick to their eating plans or program.

I created the Context Eating Method because I am done with diet culture and the temporary benefits it affords the vast majority of people.

To be honest, I didn't want to write this book because my goal is actually to get people who read weight loss books to stop reading weight loss books. That's kind of my whole point, so I agree it's a little ironic that I've put my message in a book.

I once heard you have to go where your audience is and figured it was easier to write a book than to try and befriend you in the

Starbucks drive-through or at the very-very-very back of the group fitness class we all attend twice in January and once in September.

I don't want to be another voice that adds to the noise and confusion of a six billion dollar (plus) annual industry that probably, with a few exceptions, shouldn't even exist. The last thing we need is another diet book.

We don't need to listen to another expert or jump onto another celebrity social media trend which will inevitably end when we reach the bottom of a half-melted container of chocolate chip cookie dough ice cream.

We don't need any more restrictions or self-abasement. We certainly don't need the opinion from every self-appointed diet expert in the form of your neighbor, sister-in-law, health food store employee, or 21-year-old TikTok influencer.

Is it not ironic that our North American waistlines are expanding in direct proportion to our weight loss industry? As our weight loss industry grows, our pant size grows. We are spending incredible amounts on gym memberships, diet programs, and weight loss tools, yet nothing seems to stick.

Remember, something that is not designed to be sustainable is not of much use for the long term. Temporary results are not results. They are a manipulation of specific factors for a short period of time. Anyone can lose weight if they apply enough math, exercise, restrictions, and sheer willpower. That just doesn't sound like very much fun or the way life is meant to be lived, and for most of the population, it is also completely unsustainable.

So, join me now as I walk you through a system that I have introduced to hundreds of women to help them change their relationship to food and leave the diet trap behind for good.

CHAPTER 2

THE 3 COMPONENTS

As a nutritionist, I am interested in addressing root-cause issues that lead to the symptoms my clients are experiencing. Weight gain and inability to lose weight is just one symptom that can be present within a whole cluster of symptoms. Weight gain is always suggestive of something else going on in the body.

When people choose to work with me, I look at underlying factors that can lead to weight gain and the inability to lose weight. These can include everything from blood sugar dysregulation to hormonal imbalances, digestive issues, and autoimmune diseases.

Context Eating is a tool that can be applied to anyone at any stage in life looking to improve their health and well-being over the long term. It is a healthy way of looking at food that can even be taught to our children when they are young to help them avoid diet culture altogether.

The ultimate goal of Context Eating is to place food back into its proper context in your life rather than having it be the main focus in every corner of your life. When you do this, you are leaving behind the ways our society as a whole has devalued your food experiences. Context Eating teaches you how to uplevel and enjoy your food experiences fully and healthily.

Context Eating focuses on three main concepts. These are:

1. Mindset
2. Foundational Nutrition
3. Context

This book aims to introduce you to these three concepts and help you start applying them to your everyday life. As these concepts become ingrained into your everyday habits and routines, you will begin to see your relationship with food change in ways that you never thought possible.

One of the things I hear all the time from clients working through my Context Eating Program is that their first inclinations and deeply rooted habits begin to change almost overnight. Sometimes this actually causes them a bit of distress. I have heard things like, " I WANT to WANT my donut…but now I don't even like them."

Others are in disbelief about how a firmly rooted eating pattern that was causing them to gain weight just suddenly disappears. This is why Context Eating works. It takes the constant struggle away by supporting the underlying mindset, physiological requirements of the body, and environmental factors that contribute to overeating.

PART I

MINDSET

CHAPTER 3

WHAT'S GOING ON IN THE BACKGROUND

I want to talk about some of the things that are "going on in the background" when you make certain food choices. My goal is to open your eyes to how you think about food and other areas of your life that heavily influence your actions. It is only by uncovering some of these automatic thoughts and habits that you can have a chance to make different food choices.

About three months into the COVID pandemic, my phone started ringing off the hook with people talking about the abundance of weight they had put on during the first lock-downs. There was *a lot* of associated guilt with their "quarantine fifteen" and having no energy to exercise...or to do anything at all.

There was this idea that "I should" be doing better. "I shouldn't" be eating this food. I "should" be exercising.

They didn't understand why they had so little self-control for carbs and needed so much sleep...

The obvious answer to this question was quite simply they had never lived through a pandemic before.

When we dive into this a bit deeper, we find that, at a certain level, people had slipped into "survival" mode brought on by the continuous fear indoctrination of the news cycle.

This may not have even been a conscious thing.BUT something very significant happens when things that were certain suddenly become precarious. When you are being told that there is a significant threat to our collective existence, that does something to your psyche.

When you are being told to expect food shortages and you can't always get what you need from the grocery store, alarm bells start going off in your subconscious. Even if you are not consciously concerned about the possibility of food shortage, your subconscious will pick up on the changes in your environment that suggest a threat.

Humans are primed for survival, and if there is any indication to your subconscious that the food supply is in jeopardy, you may find yourself eating everything in sight because the body knows that as long as there is a food source, you have a better chance at survival.

There is an old saying that goes, "Eat for the hunger that is coming."

If that survival mechanism has been programmed into your subconscious, you will eat as long as there is food available so that you can survive during the times when food is not available. This instinct has helped our species thrive for hundreds of thousands of years. The instinct hasn't changed, but your 24/7 access to food has, and THIS is a recipe for unhealthy weight gain.

The list of WHY you overeat is endless, and also understandable. The sad part is that most of the outside reasons you are carrying extra weight result from decisions made at the highest levels of government regarding the growing, marketing, labeling, and pricing of our food.

My point is simply that you need to see that there is a reason why your body is carrying around excess weight, and it has nothing to do with you being a bad person or your body hating you. We are going to look in detail at what some of these reasons are

So, instead of hating your body for accumulating too much fat, you will be able to understand what is going on at a really fundamental level. Hating your body never did anyone any good and simply adds to your total stress load, which in turn can lead to the inability to maintain a healthy weight.

As you make changes to your lifestyle and address some of these perceived threats, that will reduce your body's threat response and you will start to shed those protective pounds.

"Great!" you say. All I have to do is love my body, and the fat will disappear!"

"Uh-kind of, well, not really, but it's a really great start."

I don't say it is a great start lightly because it is. In the first section of this book, I will talk about the role mindset plays in successful health and body composition over the long term.

If you want to see lasting change in your outer world, you need to start by becoming more aware of your inner world. You need to become aware of your unconscious belief systems and automatic scripts, which shape your reality and all of your external outcomes.

Now before you get all dismissive and think this is all a bunch of self-actualization woo that you've heard a hundred times, I want you to know that I actually take a very practical approach to mindset that is rooted in direct cause and effect.

I want to get you to start thinking differently about the messages you hear every day about food and body image and how those impact your health and well-being. From there, you will become more aware of your inner thought processes, world beliefs, and inner dialogues that are contributing to your current state of health.

When a critical mass of people begins to think differently about their health, weight, food, and body image, we will begin to see a shift within society's broader messages about these subjects. It is at this point that permanent change will become easier for everyone.

Therefore the best place to start is simply to become aware... aware of your unconscious belief systems and automatic scripts.

Automatic scripts are the thoughts, beliefs, routines, habits, and responses that direct the vast majority of your actions. They are your default system or automated actions that help you run your day. These are important processes to help you function because if you had to think about every action you needed to take in your day, you wouldn't get far.

When a baby is learning to walk, they need to consciously concentrate on the mechanisms involved in walking. Once that process is learned, it gets transferred to muscle memory. This is how dancers dance or musicians play the piano, and this is how you go about most of your life. Once something is repeated several times, it is moved to "muscle memory" so that you don't need to think through your response or action. It happens automatically.

As an aside, individuals who are suffering from depression seem to lose some of these automated actions. That is why they can have difficulty getting up in the morning. Instead of having one automated, routine script for "getting up in the morning," they must consciously think about every little step. Sit up, stand up, turn the light on, walk to the bathroom, pick up a toothbrush, brush their teeth, etc., which is why they are often mentally exhausted only minutes into their day.

A good example of your automatic scripts is your drive to work. You don't need to consciously think through what turns you need to make or which is the best lane to be in. It is a learned behavior that you do every day that works well and saves you a lot of mental energy.

If one day you need to run an errand on your way to work, you will have to consciously remind yourself to make that detour several times or your autopilot will drive you straight to work.

And yes, this is also how you can drive to Starbucks, order your venti vanilla bean frap, double vanilla bean scoops, two pumps hazelnut syrup, half whole milk/half heavy cream, with two cake pops blended in, extra whipped cream, and chocolate sprinkles on the top, without even thinking about it.

Problems with your autopilot begin when an ingrained habit or belief is no longer in your best interest. It's like if a dancer learns the wrong choreography, they need to work intentionally and repeatedly to replace the default, learned action. When you need to replace a hard-wired habit or belief (like your 1000-calorie Starbucks order), it takes awareness, commitment, and repetition to replace the old with the new.

Awareness is the first catalyst for change. For instance, an individual must become aware that they have a substance abuse problem before they can even begin dealing with it. The same is true when it comes to your relationship with food. You must first become aware that a problem in your current way of thinking exists before you can begin to make changes.

If awareness is the first step to change, responsibility is a close second. Awareness brings to light the unconscious attitudes, beliefs, actions, and cultural norms that you were previously unaware were keeping you stuck.

Responsibility is acknowledging that you alone are accountable for your outcomes despite what negative experiences may have contributed to your current framework of belief.

Yep, taking responsibility can be a difficult process to work through.

It doesn't matter who body-shamed you, bullied you, called you fat, treated you like a second-class citizen, took advantage of your insecurities, made you listen to 10,000 food advertisements, or did something that set you up with years of disordered eating. If you want permanent change, you must let it go.

It takes a lot of courage to take the blame or excuse off another person or circumstance and fully own your situation. Most people don't initially understand that taking responsibility brings freedom because owning your outcomes moves you from a place of disempowerment to a place of empowerment.

Taking responsibility puts you back in the driver's seat of your life.

Disempowerment occurs when situations and circumstances pull you and your emotions all over the place. Disempowerment allows outside forces to determine everything from your mood, focus, health, and what you are going to eat.

Everything from the weather to the economy to your socioeconomic status to your ex-partner, world leaders, or your internet provider can be used as the scapegoat for your outcomes and cause you to eat your feelings.

This is not to say that real-life obstacles do not exist or that life is a level playing field for everyone. The starting line is not the same for everyone. The question then becomes, what do you do with what you have been given? Do you play your crappy hand and complain that the game is rigged against you, or do you find a way to turn your perceived disadvantages into something you can work with? That is the difference between an empowered and a disempowered response.

Most people hold onto their blame and excuses because it gives them a false sense of control or power. Statements such as, "It's not my fault, I am not to blame," are used as a protective measure so that you can save face and "be ok." It's not your fault you are overweight. It wasn't your failure or handling of the problem that caused your ill health. The real issue is "over there."

What people don't understand is that every time you respond with excuses and blame, what you are really saying is "I have no power." If, on an energetic level, you take no responsibility for your negative health outcomes, then, by default, you can't take credit for any of the good decisions you make, and you do not have the ability to begin to steer your life in a new direction.

Taking responsibility shifts the power from the outside circumstances to your inward resolve. Responsibility builds skills of flexibility, ingenuity, and persistence. It places a bubble between you and your circumstances so that it doesn't matter what is going on in your life; you remain in control of your outcomes. You decide how and what you are going to eat. You make a commitment to a specific way of living. You set a course, and you navigate the obstacles.

To recap, when it comes to mindset, two things must occur.

1. You must first become aware that a problem in your current way of thinking exists.
2. You must be willing to accept full responsibility for all your past and present outcomes.

So, practically what does that look like? How DO you become aware of default thoughts, beliefs, and customs that are leading to overeating?

You first need to increase your awareness of some of your default beliefs, patterns, and customs in all areas of your life, not just food.

Here is an exercise you can begin to incorporate into your day to help bring some of your default patterns and automatic scripts into your awareness.

As you go about your day today, start to catch any thoughts, words, actions, customs, and corresponding emotions that are a part of your "default mode," and make a list of them on your phone or in a journal. (See examples below for a clearer under-standing.)

Over the next few days and weeks, add any additional stories, beliefs, or customs that you become aware of that are possibly (probably) not true at all that contribute to a feeling of disempowerment or stuckness and may also be influencing how and why you are eating.

Here are some examples

- "I am useless until I have my coffee."
- "I need to do an hour of cardio."
- "Traffic is going to be terrible."
- "I've always had a sweet tooth."
- "I need to stop at Starbucks."
- "I'm menopausal, so it's impossible to lose weight."
- "Mondays are the worst"
- "It's baby weight."
- "I don't have time."
- "That has too much fat in it - I need the low-fat version."
- "It's 6 p.m.: time for a glass of wine."
- "The kids are impossible to put to bed at night."
- "If I don't eat now, I'll be hungry later."
- "I get so munchie in the evenings."
- "That's going to raise my cholesterol."
- "I can't believe I just ate that. That was so stupid."

The list of these thoughts, beliefs, and actions are endless, but try to write down as many as possible for the sake of this exercise. This will help you stop taking everything you tell yourself at face value and allow you to properly evaluate whether it is actually a truthful (or helpful) statement or belief.

The second part of this process involves questioning where these thought processes originated. Where did you "pick up" that idea? Who told you that? Why do you believe it?

There are three choices:

- Personal beliefs
- Group beliefs
- Inherited beliefs

First, personal beliefs result from personal experiences throughout your lifetime.

Some examples of personal assumptions might be,

- "I can't lose weight."
- "I am unlucky in love."
- "I am so uncoordinated."
- "I am not good at math."
- "I hate exercising."

Second, group beliefs include influences of where you live, work, the community you grew up in, and who you spend the most time with. Group beliefs often involve "us vs. them" thinking or provide unspoken pressure to maintain group norms.

Some examples of group beliefs might be,

- "Vegans are pretentious."
- "It's your turn to buy the coffee and donuts."

- "Rich people are corrupt."
- "Girls shouldn't lift."
- "Friday is cheat day."
- "We always party on the weekends."
- "Why would you want to… [ex. – eat gluten-free?] That's ridiculous."
- "We have to buy a cake for a co-worker's birthday."

Third, inherited beliefs that have been passed down from your parents and grandparents may also be a part of your wider heritage or culture. These beliefs are often subconscious and are such an ingrained part of who you are that you may have never questioned them.

- "Obesity is in our genes."
- "Women don't do that kind of work."
- "This is the way we've always done it."
- "Eat everything on your plate."

Most of us have an ancestry that includes poverty, war, struggle, famine, etc. Our ancestors were immigrants, subsistence farmers, indentured servants, slaves, or worse, and in some respects, we've never risen above the level of modern-day peasants.

So the idea of "eating for the hunger that is coming" is one of the most common inherited beliefs we see amongst our clients. Your parents or grandparents, at some point "went without." They lived in scarcity. This means that as long as there is food around and you are feeling stressed, you will continue to eat so that at some point in the future, if food becomes scarce, you have a better chance at survival.

For all the beliefs that you have added to your list, you now need to identify whether you think that belief stems from a personal belief, group belief, or an inherited belief. There may even be some that you recognize are coming from more than one source.

Identifying where a belief originated is helpful in creating space between yourself and the belief. Recognizing a false belief and then tracing it back to its origins can be a very powerful process to dismantle the hold that belief has over your life.

This is where we begin. If we can collectively begin to change these assumptions that we hold as individuals, groups, and generations, we can begin to rewrite our lives as we embrace new ideas and new truths.

When you become aware of and take responsibility for your default thoughts, beliefs and actions you are then able to choose differently. When you question the idea that, "I need to stop at Starbucks when I am running errands," you can then choose whether or not you really do "need" to stop at Starbucks, rather than it simply being an automatic habit that you do without thinking about it.

CHAPTER 4

THE REASONS YOU OVEREAT

Now that you have a bit of an understanding of how important your learned attitudes and behaviors are, it's time to focus specifically on the "whys" behind your overeating.

It's time to take a closer look at the four triggers that cause you to overeat.

Understanding these four triggers and how they influence your thoughts and actions is the next step in dismantling the habits that have brought your body to a place of ill health. Then, once you understand your triggers, you can apply some easy fixes to undo their power, start eating healthier, and permanently release the weight that you are carrying that is no longer serving you.

The four triggers that can cause you to overeat are:

- Physiological
- Emotional
- Situational
- Habitual

Physiological

Physiological triggers occur when you eat based on a cue that your body gives you because it's looking for specific nutrients. Everyone has physiological triggers that will cause them to eat or overeat.

Physiological triggers are the most important to identify because it's much more difficult to address emotional, situational, or habitual overeating if the physiological needs of the body are not being met.

There are many symptoms that are indicators of nutrient deficiencies, and craving or binge eating certain foods is one of them. Our body requires specific nutrients to help us achieve optimum health. One of the most common things our body craves is fat and fat-soluble vitamins because we use fat in every cell of our body. Fat is also essential for hormone production.

When we do not have enough good fats in our diet, our body will signal us to eat fatty foods. Unfortunately, most of the fatty foods that are readily available to us are not necessarily healthy and are also loaded with sugar or refined carbohydrates.

Craving chips, french fries, desserts, hamburgers, and pizza often has more to do with your body needing fat and less to do with you craving salt or carbohydrates. There are many other nutrients that your body may crave, including protein, B vitamins, vitamin C, protein, iron, magnesium, and more.

Understanding this "why" behind your cravings will help you to give your body what it actually needs. When you begin to eat enough healthy fats, protein and other vital nutrients, you will help support the physiological needs of the body, which will reduce cravings that are triggered by nutrient deficiencies.

One of the best ways we have learned to get rid of cravings and stop binge eating is to add fats like avocado, olive oil, fatty fish, nuts, seeds, and coconut oil, and high-quality protein sources to your daily diet. You can also take supplements where necessary to help support other nutrient deficiencies. Unlike "weight loss supplements," these supplements give you the nutrients that your body is missing so that you stop wanting to eat everything in sight.

For more information on which supplements I recommend, read Chapter 15

Physiological cravings need to be addressed before you can have long-term success mastering the other triggers. This is why it is first on the list of areas we address with our clients and is foundational to how we set up our menu planning.

Emotional

Emotional triggers occur when you eat based on an emotional cue causing you to believe eating will bring increased feelings of happiness or connection.

Many people have emotional triggers that will cause them to eat or overeat. These triggers are usually fairly easy to identify once you become aware of them.

In the same way that you have physiological needs that must be met, you also have emotional needs that must be met. When you are consciously or unconsciously not getting your emotional needs met, you begin compensating through food because eating certain foods will trigger some of the same feel-good neurotransmitters and hormones that bonding, connection, and healthy relationships provide.

In addition to healthy relationships, healthy touch, including sexual and non-sexual touch, are incredibly important for your health. If there is a lack of touch in your life, you may also compensate with food.

The other thing I often see is people who have either positive or negative associations with food related to their parents or caregivers. If you grew up being shown love or reward from your parents through food, you would naturally look to specific foods to continue to connect with those feelings of validation and love.

Conversely, if your parents shamed your eating, appetite, and food choices or somehow restricted your food, there can be an emotional attachment to food that is related more towards regaining your sense of control.

Emotional triggers for eating may require a multifaceted approach to reduce your impact on disordered eating. However, awareness of those triggers can be incredibly powerful as it allows you to begin questioning your food choices and contexts in an observational, nonjudgmental way.

The final thing that needs to be addressed when talking about emotional eating is to become aware of emotional or morality-based language around food. This is extremely common, and you may need to work hard to change your language around food.

Words like "good," "bad," or "cheat" should never be used in conjunction with food choices. Equating food choices with morality is one of the ways that you can get locked into a negative cycle of emotional eating.

Sure, there are better and worse choices when it comes to eating, but what we focus on with Context Eating is realizing that the context the food is eaten in is more important than the food itself. This mental switch is one of the foundational aspects of our Context Eating Method and can lead to incredible breakthroughs when it comes to destructive emotional attachments to food. We will be discussing more about this in later chapters.

Situational

Situational triggers occur when you eat based on situational cues that you receive from your environment. Situational triggers occur when you are presented with specific situations that are associated with certain foods or food quantities. Identifying these triggers allows you to make informed food decisions.

Situational triggers are sneaky because they can seem like legitimate reasons for indulging or potentially not making the best choices. Some situations are perfect for eating a bit more than you normally would or indulging in something extra tasty, but other situations are not, so this is where it becomes important to evaluate your situational eating.

Eating out with family or friends and celebrating a loved one's birthday is a great time for cake and decadent food. On the other hand, feeling obligated to have a piece of overly sweet store-bought cake every week in the lunchroom because another one of your 63 coworkers is having a birthday may not be the best time to indulge.

Less-than-ideal situations include eating takeout for your entire business trip when those business trips are happening every other week or having to finish that fifteen-dollar dessert because you paid for it. How many of you have felt the need to grab seconds at the buffet so that you get your money's worth even if you're not hungry? Yessss…that's what I thought!

Situational triggers are things you need to consciously walk into and decide ahead of time what your response to the trigger will be. Think about which situations are negotiable and which are non-negotiable for you. Are you okay skipping out on Bob-from-accounting's cake celebration in the office lunchroom? Then skip it. Never feel obligated to eat something.

Habitual

Habitual triggers occur when you eat based on subconscious cues, routines, or patterns that you do not challenge.

Habitual triggers are things that can sometimes be the hardest to pick up on initially but are often the things that, with even a little bit of focus, you can begin to turn around for the better.

Habitual triggers are the things that you do on autopilot. They are the things that you do with food that you don't even consciously think about. An example of a common habitual trigger is stopping at the drive-through window to pick up a snack while you are out running errands.

You don't stop and ask yourself if you are actually hungry and need a snack; it's just something you do because you're out.

You have pizza on Friday nights whether you want pizza or not.

You munch away on the food that you're cooking for supper, and by the time supper is made, you have eaten an extra half a portion.

You pour yourself a glass of wine or two because it's wine o'clock.

You grab a bag of chips or chocolate when you sit down to watch TV.

You take the same portion size of food that you always take no matter how hungry you are.

You eat at the same time of day, no matter how hungry you are.

You grab a snack on your break at work because what else would you do on your break?

Habitual triggers can have a range of holds on you. Some are easy to let go of once you become aware of them; others are much more difficult.

The way we deal with habitual triggers within the Context Eating Method is by starting with the path of least resistance. Start with what is easy and then move on to the more difficult things.

Even making small changes to your patterns can make a huge difference in your health and approach to food, and it's the accumulation of small changes that is going to make the biggest difference long term.

This also allows for space to NOT need to completely try and remake yourself overnight. If we go back to our "I'll Start Monday" scenarios where you are literally trying to change everything about yourself overnight, we have learned this approach does not work.

The other really important thing to recognize is that diets focus only on trying to get you to change your HABITS, which is why they don't work.

It is very difficult to break your real-world habits until you become aware of and address the physiological, emotional, and situational triggers that cause you to overeat. In the Context Eating Method, we start with the physiological triggers and work our way inward toward the habitual.

Once the physiological triggers are addressed, the emotional triggers become easier to handle. Once the emotional triggers are addressed, the situational triggers become easier to manage. Once the situational triggers are addressed, many of the habitual triggers simply fall away.

This is a much different approach than depending on sheer willpower and determination.

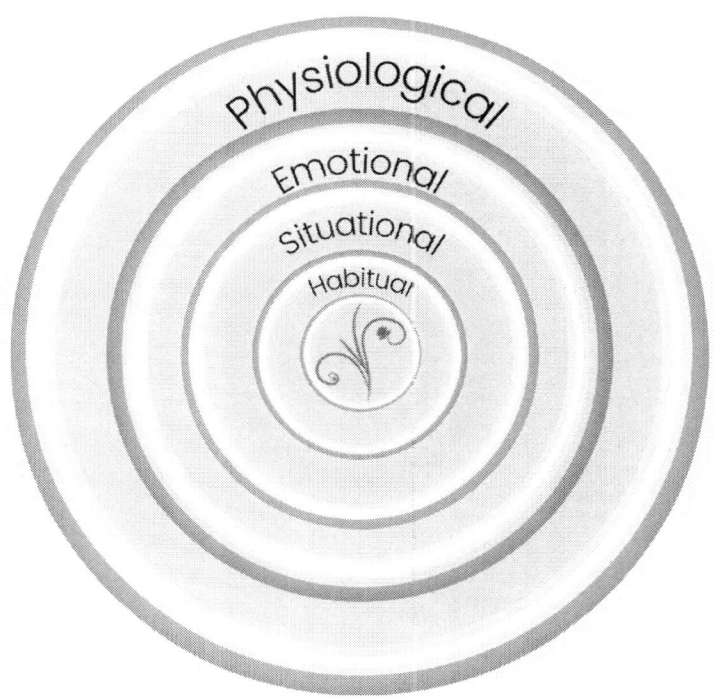

Becoming more aware of and understanding all your triggers can help you permanently lose unwanted weight by putting food back into its proper context.

Understanding your triggers is a completely different way of looking at and managing disordered eating. It does not involve calorie counting, restrictive eating or all-or-nothing approaches and instead looks at the why behind the behavior.

Fixing the WHY (ie getting to the root cause of the behavior) is a much easier way to change the outcome. The alternative requires an incredible amount of discipline and fighting natural inclinations. This leaves you feeling deprived and is not something sustainable for most people.

To help you identify the areas where you need the most focus, go to www.luckybookpublishing.com/contexteating and download the Triggered Eating Inventory. This short quiz will help you identify the areas that are most influencing your disordered eating and help you become more aware of the outside forces that are influencing your overeating.

CHAPTER 5

BEGINNING WHERE YOU ARE

One of the first statements I have heard people say over and over again when they decide that they need to make some changes is, "I don't even know where to start." They will follow up that statement by letting me know about the hundred different weight-loss approaches and philosophies, new fad diets, and MLM groups they have tried in the past without success.

It is important to note that when I say "without success," that is their own interpretation of their experience. I don't see any past attempt at health as a failure. The question I like to ask people when they recite all their "failed" attempts, and unsuccessful lines of treatment is: "but what have you learned?"

Surprisingly (more to them than me), they have learned SO MUCH on their health journey and have a lot of information that they can now apply to their current situation.

For instance, they will say things like:

- "I know I will not eat kale – I hate kale."
- "I have trouble eating breakfast in the morning."
- "I often forget to drink my water, but when I do, I feel so much better."
- "I need a menu plan that works for my whole family."
- "I need someone to just tell me what to do."
- "I have a whole cupboard of supplements that I never take."
- "If I don't exercise first thing in the morning, it won't happen."
- "When I get outside daily, my mood is really improved."
- "Once I go a few days without sugar, I don't crave it anymore."
- "I love broccoli and most other vegetables."
- "A smoothie in the morning works really well for me."
- "I can't keep junk food in the house or I will eat it all."
- "Going off coffee makes me constipated."
- "When I get 8 hours of sleep I feel amazing."
- "I can eat a bit of dairy, but if I eat a lot, I get a headache."
- "When it is rainy, my pain goes way up."
- "I hate protein shakes"
- "My thyroid tests always come back normal"
- "I loved my cardio kickboxing class."
- "After I did an elimination diet, I noticed I felt better when I didn't eat dairy."

The list of what people have learned about themselves and their health after trying a program, new routine, or even a new fad diet are endless. Instead of looking at these past actions as failed attempts to fix whatever the problem was, you need to start looking at them as the wealth of information these years of self-attention and care have given you.

So the answer to "where do I begin" is to begin where you are. It's not at the beginning. It's not standing on a pile of failed attempts. It's standing on the mountain of information, experimentation, experiences, and outcomes that you already know to be true and then moving forward from there.

Framing your past effort towards greater health as a failure does such a disservice to the person you have become and all the previous investments you have made in yourself. If you want to move forward with confidence and assurance in your next steps, you need to reaffirm to yourself that:

- That program was not a wrong decision.
- That gym membership wasn't a waste of money
- That product wasn't a scam.
- That new piece of exercise equipment was not in vain.
- All those tests and appointments were not a waste of time.

And anybody or voice telling you differently or pointing out all the unused products, programs, gym memberships, and unused workout gear lining your closet needs to be given a gentle "shhh" as you gather up all the lessons learned and focus on your next step.

This is why you will hear me talk a lot about honoring your journey. We are not all in the same place and the reality is you will never arrive at a place of perfection. You need to stop looking at health as a destination and instead look at it as a series of imperfect steps that will lead you closer to your goal. You need to put away the idea of decisions you make being wrong or right moves and instead focus on what the accumulation of experiences have taught you.

This is not to say that everything that you have done in the name of your health has been ultimately "good" for you, and some of the attempts you have made and the people you have listened to may have indeed caused some setbacks. However, it is important to understand that whatever decisions you made in the past were done with the information and ability you had at hand. You cannot judge your past actions through the lenses of today's experience and access to knowledge.

In honoring your journey, you must forgive yourself, acknowledge that you were doing the best you were able to do at the time, and recognize that when you are living purposefully, you are always moving forward in knowledge, understanding, and acceptance of yourself and others. In this way, you will remain open to new ideas, better ways of doing things, evolving science, and the recognition of your own growth and life stages.

The collection of any information, whether it is hard data from a laboratory, symptom analysis, or a big, long list of things you know haven't worked for you in the past, gives you a huge head start in helping to determine what your next steps are.

Beginning where you are requires some self-analysis and the strength to admit that you are not where you want to be. It requires taking stock of all the information you have already gathered so that you can formulate your own path to wellness that is not a fad or a temporary fix, but a permanent solution that you can live with for life.

So take what you have learned and apply it. If you hate kale, stop eating kale. If you know your mental health depends on you getting outside every day for a walk, prioritize your walks. If a protein shake in the morning works for you, stop forcing yourself to eat eggs.

Yes, there will always be things that we can work on and improve. If you hate ALL vegetables and will only eat peanut butter on toast, you will need to challenge yourself to expand your horizons. The point is not to allow perceived obstacles such as, "I hate fish" or "I can't get through the day without an iced coffee" to stand in your way of getting started.

My goal is to take you from struggling and being unsure of your next steps to a place that works for you. I want to help you ensure your body has everything it needs to release unwanted weight and transform your health.

CHAPTER 6

PREPARING YOUR ENVIRONMENT

One of the foundations of Context Eating is the importance of up-leveling your food experience. Our fast-paced modern society has devalued food to the point that it has become whatever you can shove into your face in the quickest and least labor-intensive way possible. This is why fast food is a staple in most households.

As you will learn as you work through the various components of Context Eating, you will start to become more aware of how devalued your food experience has become and how this directly contributes to your inability to keep your weight and body composition at healthy levels.

Have you ever seen the TV series "Downton Abbey?" If you have watched the series you will know that every meal they ate was an art form. From the way they dressed, to the presentation, to the etiquette, to which spoon was for which part of the meal – every aspect of every meal was deliberate.

Now, I'm not asking you to recreate "Downton Abbey," but there is something to be said for elevating your food experience. Instead of inhaling a Wendy's burger in the car or grabbing a handful of chips out of the bag and eating them over the sink, there is a different energy to the food that is ingested in a more intentional manner. There is a time and place and a way to eat that I believe can begin to put food back into its proper context in your life.

I understand hectic, busy schedules don't always allow for this type of formal food preparation, and sometimes a Wendy's burger on the way to practice may be the best choice that you have in the moment, but I also know that when you become more intentional with your food environment, preparation, and consumption, it can set the stage for changing the trajectory of your health.

The ideas in this chapter can help you organize and set you up for success, but it is important to note that not everything will be applicable to everyone.

Below I have created a checklist that considers some things you may not have thought about in regards to setting up your food environment for success.

Now let me be clear to any of you who are already living in overwhelm – the point of this checklist is to give you ideas that may work for you. This is not meant to be an exhaustive list of more things you need to do or check off to have an acceptable food environment and start learning how to incorporate Context Eating into your life.

If this feels insurmountable, simply choose a couple of the ideas on the list that you think might work for you and leave the rest. This is just really about getting you to start thinking about your food environment and intake in a different way.

- Clean out and organize your kitchen pantry and cupboards. Get rid of old/stale food, things past their best-before date, and things you bought but never used.
- Do the same for the fridge and freezer. Get rid of old condiments and things that have been hanging around too long: freezer-burnt items and things you know you will never eat.
- Clean out your produce drawers, wash out any grossness, and wipe down the shelves of the fridge.
- If you have a "supplement cupboard," do the same thing. Remove old protein powders, expired products, and anything that you have no idea what it does or why you bought it in the first place.
- Go through your cupboards and identify some of your favorite foods that you feel are leading to weight gain or poor health. Don't do anything with them. Don't throw them out unless you want to. Just consciously acknowledge that they are not helping you reach your goals.
- Organize your food left-over containers, making sure they have lids or that lids have containers.
- Sharpen your knives, or if you don't have any good knives go out and buy yourself a nice knife or two.
- Get a nice cutting board if you don't have one.
- Replace your old dishcloths and towels.

- Clear away any clutter, like papers/bills, etc., from your kitchen area.
- Keep your countertops as clear as possible.
- If you have a nice set of dishes you never use, get them out and use them instead of the cheaper stuff you bought so the kids wouldn't break the good stuff.
- When you go to eat, use the nice dishes and set the table; no more eating at the counter or in front of the TV.
- When eating at the table, remove any work-related items such as laptops/phones/papers, etc.
- Consider buying an instant pot or slow cooker that can help you with meal planning.
- Become aware of background noise like the news, negatively themed TV shows, or video games that are contributing to unconscious stress.

Some of you will look at this list and think, "This is easy, and I've already done most of this already." For some, this list will feel impossible and impractical. For others, you may look at this list and dismiss it as irrelevant to what you are trying to achieve in terms of weight loss.

Those are all valid responses. If you have already done most of this and your food environment is in an okay place, fantastic, that is one more asset in your favor. If you are looking at this list and thinking this is impossible, I hear you. Choose a couple of the easiest things to do that you think will make the most impact for you and leave the others. If you are dismissing this list as irrelevant or not a priority, I would ask you to consider why you think that and suggest that you humor me a bit and do at least a couple of things on the list.

Investing a bit of time, energy, and money into your kitchen space will automatically set the intention that you are wanting to elevate your food experience. Preparing food when you have sharp knives versus the set you got for $10 at Ikea makes even cutting up vegetables more enjoyable.

Using fancy dishes brings a different energy to the table than eating off the cheap plates. Ensuring that there are no papers or screens in the eating area helps to focus the attention on the food, which once again offers a different food experience. Even if you are having chicken nuggets and Kraft dinner for supper, you can still treat that meal with an intention and a thankfulness that ensures you never take food for granted.

It is giving the meal the space and time in your life that it warrants vs. being something you do as quickly as possible without much thought. Setting this example for your children at an early age can make a big difference as they grow up and help them learn proper food contexts.

Yes, I know, for some, this is all going to seem impractical and off base, but I know without a doubt that the intention you give to something is important, and that is why even treating a meal of boxed mac-n-cheese with some reverence is important.

Again, this should not be done as a chore or another stress point in your life. It may be that up-leveling your food experience is going to take some time to implement in your house. It may mean that only a couple of meals per week are eaten at the table because, currently, all of your meals are eaten in the car on the way to hockey practice.

It might mean that YOU are the only one eating at the table with the nice dishes because that is just not something your family does and your teenagers are not having it. So I want to remind you to take the path of least resistance. This may not be the hill you want to die on, but if you want to transform your health and release unwanted weight from your body, this process can make a huge difference.

To recap: setting up your environment for success can be a very helpful process as you begin to learn how to Context Eat. So, review the above checklist, do what you feel is useful and helpful, and leave the rest.

PART II

FOUNDATIONAL NUTRITION

CHAPTER 7

THE IMPORTANCE OF HYDRATION AND ITS LINK TO YOUR SUCCESS

So far we have discussed the importance of mindset and how it works as a foundation for improving your eating contexts. Mindset supports the changes you want to make to your environment and how you view the role of food in your life as a whole.

Now we need to move from thought into action. I am using the word action to represent your real-life choices: in this case, your hydration and nutrition. It is not enough to know and understand your triggers and underlying factors driving your disordered relationship with food. You need concrete actions that you can implement to 1. Address your physiological food triggers, and 2. Learn which foods are going to give you the biggest support when it comes to steering your health in the right direction.

In our Context Eating Program, hydration is a focus that I make a priority for all of my clients the very first day they start working with me. For me, hydration actually bridges the gap between mindset and nutrition. Let me explain what I mean by that.

Some of my clients initially roll their eyes at me because they don't want to believe that something as simple as drinking more water can have a serious impact on their health and ability to drop unwanted weight.

They want me to get to the good stuff. The secret sauce, the low carbs, the supplements, the exercise that is going to suddenly change everything for them. How could something that is free and so readily available to everyone make such a difference? If drinking more water was the key to keeping off unwanted weight…shouldn't we all be skinny?

Here's the thing about hydration…

Time and time again, my clients who make hydration an ongoing priority are the ones who not only see improvements in many areas of their health, but they also stay the course and find it easier to implement other healthy changes into their lives.

I believe that focusing on increasing your hydration works like a gateway to establishing other healthy habits and making them stick.

It is part of the foundation of forming healthy habits. If you can't do this simple, readily available, free, low effort, low barrier, and high reward habit, then your ability to stick to other habits come into question.

The benefits of making adequate hydration a part of your day go far beyond the actual hydrating aspects and start building your habit-forming resolve.

Without this resolve, you can have all the information in the world but not possess the ability to take consistent action in the direction of your goals.

This is why I say that hydration is the link between mindset and nutrition. Focusing on your water intake involves a much simpler mindset and lifestyle shift than altering your diet. Getting good at the easy, low-barrier habits will make implementing some of the more difficult habits easier.

Everything about Context Eating is to make changes easier to implement. That is why I start with the simple things before moving on to the more challenging things.

So now that you understand the mindset benefits of water, let's take a look at all the other reasons you want to increase your hydration.

The first thing you need to understand is that proper hydration is not just essential for humans but for almost every life form, if not every life form, on the planet.

There is a reason that those who are looking for life on other planets are obsessed with figuring out whether or not a planet contains or did contain a source of water. Water is vital to life as we know it.

This is important to understand because you would think that if proper hydration is essential to all life, it would be one of the

FIRST areas that doctors look at when evaluating an individual's health status. But unless hydration is out of balance to the extreme, i.e. a person is extremely dehydrated, it is not a first go-to when considering how to improve health outcomes.

And this is where it is important to avoid looking at things as black and white/yes or no.

The answer to "is this person dehydrated" is not simply YES or NO. Hydration should be looked at on a spectrum. There is complete dehydration on one end of the spectrum and optimum hydration on the other end. But there is also a whole spectrum in the middle where people may fall. Therefore, if you are far enough away from "optimum," it could be considered a contributing factor to your inability to lose and keep off unwanted weight.

Consider a plant. When a plant is noticeably dehydrated, it looks like it's dead but amazingly, when you add a little bit of water, it perks right back up. We are not that different from plants. When you feel crappy, fatigued, and even depressed, your first thought should be, "have I had enough water to drink today?"

- Our body is more than 60% water
- Our brain is more than 75% water
- Our blood is more than 90% water

Proper hydration supports the whole body, your brain, and your blood.

For the BODY, water is vital for the following functions:

- Water supports digestive processes performed by the liver, bowels, and kidneys. For example, one of the first things you should do if you are constipated is to drink more water.
- Water boosts skin health and beauty by hydrating skin cells and helping to ensure the proper elimination of toxins from the body. Our skin mirrors what is happening inside our body, so if we have rashes or acne, it can mean there is a buildup of toxins.
- Water keeps joints and cartilage lubricated, reducing pain and inflammation If you have pain conditions, you need to drink more water. For many people, simply drinking more water can substantially lower their pain levels.
- Water helps to regulate homeostasis, including blood pressure, electrolytes, and core body temperature.
- And finally, water assists with weight loss as it supports the liver and elimination processes. It also helps to curb appetite, regulate mood, and keep your energy up. All of these things can contribute to maintaining a healthy weight. When you are dehydrated, your body can sometimes send signals to eat rather than drink, so staying well-hydrated can also eliminate the physiological urge to snack between meals.

For the BRAIN, water is vital for the following functions:

- Water improves cognition and focus, so drink more water if you are experiencing brain fog.
- Water assists communication throughout your nervous system.
- Water balances your mood and emotions, which can help reduce emotional eating.
- Water can prevent and relieve headaches.

For the BLOOD, water is vital for the following functions:

- Water improves the flow of oxygen through your body which increases energy.
- Water increases blood flow to your brain, increasing mental alertness and cognition.
- Water is also a main component of lymph fluid, which is a vital part of your immune function.
- So one of the first questions I always get asked is, "How much water should I be drinking?"

This will vary from person to person based on things like activity level, rate of water output, and how much coffee you drink, but two good rules of thumb are:

If you are trying to lose weight, drink more than what you think you need (i.e., don't wait until you get thirsty).

A good general guideline is to take your weight in pounds, divide it by two, and that is the number of ounces you should aim for.

E.g. 150lb/2 = 75 oz of water.

Now, if you have significant weight to lose, I don't want you trying to get in 18 or more glasses of water. Make a goal that is reasonable for you. I suggest 10-12 glasses or 80 oz. The last thing I want is for you to get discouraged before you even begin. The point of the calculation is simply to show water intake should vary by weight.

Some additional considerations for when you are trying to get in an optimum amount of water are:

- Increase your intake of water if you also drink coffee or alcohol.
- Increase your intake if you exercise or sweat.

One final tip that you need to consider when you increase your water intake is to make sure that you also take in more salt. A Celtic, Himalayan sea salt or an electrolyte replacement is what I suggest. This last tip can be really important, especially once you reduce your sodium intake because you have cut out processed foods. Sometimes people in ill health who start drinking a lot more water feel worse than they did before they started increasing their water. Adding in a salt or electrolyte replacement can help ensure proper electrolyte balance.

In conclusion, even being mildly dehydrated can affect the efficiency of how your body runs, processes toxins, repairs, and rebuilds, as well as your ability to lose weight. Sometimes the answer to a problem is not difficult. Sometimes if you do the most basic thing, you can reduce your symptoms and improve your health.

My suggestion is that while you are learning about the rest of the Context Eating Method and planning out how to incorporate it into your life, you do nothing else except focus on getting to your optimum hydration levels. Make that your sole goal for at least two weeks before you begin to incorporate anything else. Get really good at this and take the time to work out any issues you are having (like running to the bathroom or getting up often at night). These side effects should begin to slow down after your body adjusts.

I know most people want to jump right into the whole Context Eating system the very first day, but remember, Context Eating is not a diet. The goal is to replace dieting, which means that you must come at it with a different approach. Slower implementation and changing foundational habits are part of the process to help you avoid the idea of "quick fixes" and fads.

Here are my top tips for getting more water into your day:

1. Start your day off with a big glass of water. Make that the first thing you do in the morning.
2. Measure out the water you want to drink into a 1-liter container. I personally like to use a 1-liter glass mason jar. This makes it easier to keep track of how much you are drinking.
3. Keep your water within reach. If it is the easiest thing to grab, you will be more likely to choose it.

4. Drink herbal teas or add lemon to your water to break up the monotony.

5. Stop drinking your water within 90 minutes of bed to avoid getting up many times at night.

CHAPTER 8

THE CONTEXT EATING MEAL PLAN

If you just bought this book and skipped immediately to this chapter, please go back and read the previous sections to understand the foundational components of Context Eating. I know you just want to get to the meat of the program so you can get started. I totally get it, but the mindset component, and especially the chapter on triggers, is so important to understand. So please promise me you'll go back and read them before beginning the program.

The Context Eating Meal Plan is the easiest way to structure your meals to help you lose weight, maintain your weight loss, and improve your overall health and well-being. I made it as simple as possible to follow and incorporate into your life.

There are four food catagories, and the goal is to properly incorporate these into your life in a sustainable and healthy way.

In this chapter, I will talk about catagories one through three and leave discussions around catagory four until chapter 11 and onward, when we do a deep dive into the CONTEXT portion of the Context Eating Method.

1. Catagory One: Focus Foods
2. Category Two: Satiating Foods
3. Catagory Three: Comfort Foods
4. Catagory Four: Context Foods

In this chapter, I will teach you about the different food catagories and how easy it is to incorporate the concepts of the Context Eating Meal Plan into your day. I will also teach you how to put together your own balanced meals using the Context Eating Method format, examples, and recipes. I will give you everything you need to easily create your personalized eating plan.

I do this rather than handing you a ready-to-go menu, so your menu plan is 100% your own and includes your favorite foods that work for you and your family.

Working through this chapter will teach you to put together nutritionally balanced meals so you can apply this skill to the rest of your life rather than depending on others to figure this out for you.

This is important if you find yourself in a situation or life circumstance where you suddenly need to be flexible with your food choices to figure out your best options.

This also eliminates the problem of hating what's on your menu plan. The whole point of Context Eating is to show you how to eat all your favorite foods in a way that won't lead to continued weight gain.

First, let's first go through what this meal plan IS NOT and what IT IS.

After working in this industry for as long as I have, I believe that Context Eating is the best way to eat for most people. It is not calorie restricted. It does not limit food groups except for refined carbohydrates. It is not vegetarian, but it is possible to follow it if you are a vegetarian. It does not require specialized foods, and it does not require you to count anything. No calories, no carbs, no macros.

Instead, it is a balanced way of eating nutrient-dense foods to support blood sugar regulation, gut health, liver health, and hormone health. This, in turn, will lead to better health outcomes and the loss of unhealthy weight.

The first catagory is your focus foods.

Focus foods are foundational foods that I would like you to incorporate at every meal you eat.

While all foods in the menu plan have great nutrient profiles, the foods I have deemed focus foods contain a lot of antioxidants, fiber, phytonutrients, pre and probiotics, and anti-inflammatory properties. These foods are supportive of digestion and the liver.

Many of them, like cruciferous vegetables, have properties that can help support the reduction of symptoms associated with dysregulated hormones. Others, like herbs and spices, have their own unique health properties. For instance, cinnamon can support blood sugars and turmeric is a potent anti-inflammatory.

There are several categories of focus foods, and the goal is to incorporate a minimum of two types at each meal. These should be the foods that the rest of your meal is built around. There is no limit on focus foods. Eat what you feel is right for you.

List of focus foods:

▷ **Vegetables**

- Arugula
- Asparagus
- Beets
- Peppers
- Bok Choy
- Broccoli
- Brussel Sprouts
- Cabbage
- Carrots
- Cauliflower
- Celery
- Collard greens
- Cucumber
- Dandelion

- Eggplant
- Fennel
- Green beans
- Kale
- Leaks
- Mushrooms
- Okra
- Kholrabi
- Onions
- Parsnips
- Radish
- Lettuce
- Sauerkraut
- Spinach
- Sprouts
- Swiss Chard
- Tomatoes
- Turnip
- Watercress
- Zucchini
- Other nonstarchy vegetables

▷ Superfoods

- Apple Cider Vinegar
- Bone Broth
- Lemon
- Lime
- Green tea
- Herbal teas

- Moringa
- Spirulina
- Inulin Fiber
- Acacia Fiber
- Shirataki/Konjac Noodles
- *Berries

▷ **Herbs and Spices:**

- Cayenne
- Cilantro
- Cinnamon
- Garlic
- Ginger
- Mint
- Oregano
- Parsley
- Rosemary
- Sage
- Sea Salt
- Turmeric
- Thyme
- Fenugreek
- Basil

Please note this is not an exhaustive list. If you know that a food contains high nutrient density, high fiber, low-calorie value or has some other medicinal quality, it is probably a Focus Food.

Focus on adding good amounts of these foods to every meal you consume.

*Note - We consider berries a superfood, due to the amount of antioxidants and fiber they contain. However they also contain natural sugars so aim for ½ cup or less per serving.

The second category of food in the Context Eating menu plan is the satiating foods.

These foods are either high in protein, high in healthy fats, or both. Yes of course, fats and proteins are two very different things. However, it was easier to combine them under one banner as satiating foods, as many foods contain decent amounts of both fats and proteins.

Proteins and healthy fats have very different roles in the body, but one of the things that they both do is create feelings of fullness and satiety. Feeling full and satisfied makes you less likely to engage in disordered eating or have uncontrollable cravings. They also do not cause blood sugar levels to fluctuate in the same way that carbohydrates do. Adding protein and fat to each meal is the second thing I want to see when you build out your meal plan. Again, I am not focusing on portion sizes because your body should naturally become satiated when you eat the right amount of these foods. Experiment a bit. Listen to your hunger cues. Eat until you feel satisfied but not uncomfortably full.

List of satiating foods

▷ **Proteins:**

- Beef -ground
- Beef -lean
- Canned fish
- Chicken
- Eggs
- Fish and Seafood
- Game
- Ham
- Lamb
- Lean Pork
- Protein powder
- Tempeh
- Turkey

▷ **Fats:**

- Avocado
- Avocado oil
- Butter
- Flaxseed oil
- Ghee
- Heavy cream
- MCT oil
- Olive oil
- Olives
- Mayo

- Coconut oil
- Salad dressing
- Coconut meat
- Coconut cream

▷ **Combination Protein/Fat:**

- Bacon
- Cheese -Hard
- Cheese - Cottage
- Kefir
- Milk -homogenized
- Nut butters
- Seed butter
- Sour cream
- Yogurt - Full fat Greek-plain

▷ **Nuts:** Almonds

- Brazil
- Cashews
- Hazelnuts
- Macadamia
- Pecans
- Pistachio
- Walnuts

▷ **Seeds:** Chia

- Flax
- Hemp
- Pumpkin
- Sunflower

The third catagory of food in the Context Eating menu plan is your comfort foods.

These are your carbohydrates. Now when you are looking to lose weight, I would suggest that you only have 2-3 choices from this list per day. This means that you may not want to include comfort food at every meal. The choice is yours.

While I would suggest that the balance of your meals are filled with items from catagory 1 and catagory 2, everyone has different needs when it comes to the amount of carbohydrates they add to their menu. These complex carbohydrates will add in additional fiber and antioxidants and contain many of the "comfort foods" we have become used to.

Use the suggested portion sizes as a guide, not a standard for right or wrong. As a general rule, most people are used to having much bigger portions of things like bread, pasta, or rice, so when you look at these portion sizes, these may be much smaller than you are used to.

The Standard American Diet is very carb-heavy, and you have been taught that eight cups of spaghetti is a normal portion size for pasta. It's not. Neither is a potato the size of your face. I have given you portion size guidelines, not to restrict you, but to teach you what a portion size of carbs actually is.

List of comfort foods

▷ **Fruit**

- Apple 1 small
- Bananas ½
- Watermelon 1/2 cup
- Cherries 1/2 cup
- Dates 1/4 cup
- Grapefruits ½
- Grapes 12 grapes
- Mango 1
- Melon 1/2 cup
- Oranges 1 small
- Peach 1 small
- Pear 1 small
- Pineapple 1/2 cup
- Plums 1
- Pomegranate ½

▷ **Grain/Starch/Sugar**

- Barley (cooked)1/2 cup
- Beans (kidney/Navy etc.) 1/2 cup
- Black Strap Molasses 2 Tbsp
- Bread - 1 slice

- Bagel 1/2
- English Muffin ½
- Bread- tortilla wraps – 1x 6inch
- Cereal- high fiber 1/2 cup
- Chocolate- Dark - 25 grams
- Corn 1/2 cup
- Cream of wheat 1/2 cup
- Granola 1/2 cup
- Honey 2 Tbsp
- Hummus 1/2 cup
- Lentils 1/2 cup
- Maple syrup 2 Tbsp
- Oatmeal (not instant) cooked 1/2 cup
- Oat Milk 1 cup
- Pasta 1/2 cup
- Peas 1/2 cup
- Popcorn 1/4 cup unpopped
- Potatoes 1/2 a medium
- Quinoa 1/2 cup
- Rice - 1/2 cup
- Crackers 6 crackers
- Squash 1/2 cup
- Sweet potato 1/2 cup
- Tortilla Chips -12

The last category of foods that you need to know about is your Context Foods.

Although we are not going to discuss adding your Context Foods to your menu plan yet, I do want to list them out here for you so that when you read about how to add them to your meals in subsequent chapters, you can come back to the list here.

Context Foods are the foods that you enjoy for the experience. They are the foods you celebrate, treat yourself with, or indulge in. They are often high in sugar or contain little to no nutrient value. They may be very high in calories or have a combination of ingredients that are not conducive to health. Or, they may just be something you need to set some boundaries around. I call them Context Foods because these foods should ideally only be eaten in certain contexts.

List of Context Foods

▷ **Baked goods**

- Muffins
- Cookies
- Pies
- Cakes
- Cheesecakes
- Bread

▷ **Candy and chocolate**

- Chocolate bars
- Gummy bears
- Lollipops
- Halloween candy

▷ **High sugar/calorie drinks**

- Soda
- Juice
- Beer
- Wine
- Coolers
- High-calorie coffees
- Hot chocolate
- Milkshakes

▷ **Snacks**

- Chips
- Pretzels
- Crackers
- Granola bars

▷ **Heavy carbs**

- Pizza
- Pasta
- French fries
- Poutine
- Ice cream
- Nachos
- Pancakes
- Waffles
- High sugar/low fiber cereals
- Casseroles

- Lasagna

Understanding the differences between your focus foods, satiating foods, comfort foods, and context foods is a first step because it helps identify the foods you will use in your menu plan frequently.

Recap

The Context Eating Meal Plan is a simple combination of foods from four categories. In this chapter, we have only introduced you to the first three catagories and will incorporate the fourth, Context Foods, in a later chapter.

Your goal in this section is simply to choose foods from catagory 1, 2, and sometimes 3 at each meal that you eat. For instance, one of your meals might look like steamed broccoli (focus), asparagus (focus) with melted butter or olive oil (satiating), chicken (satiating), and half a cup of quinoa (comfort).

Don't like quinoa or broccoli? Choose different vegetables and starches from the list. The whole point of this menu plan is not to overhaul absolutely everything you are eating. It is to help you put together better combinations of the foods you already eat every day.

I would encourage you to try new foods you don't normally eat, but the ultimate goal of Context Eating is to make your meal plan as sustainable as possible while teaching you how to incorporate all the foods you love.

Eventually, you should be able to get to a point where you don't need to formally plan your meals. You can just put meals together using this four-catagory system without thinking too hard about it. That's the goal. This way of eating becomes so automatic that you don't need to spend much time and energy thinking about how to combine foods for greater nutrition and balanced blood sugars.

To help you get started, I have created a **Bonus Section** at the end of this book and given you links to online tools that you can use to help you create your personalized menu plan. These include:

- Darpan's favorite family recipes
- 20 examples of breakfasts, lunches, suppers, and snacks to help you create your own menu plan

These are all nutrient-dense, filling recipes that should leave you feeling full and satiated.

Please take some time to review the recipes and choose some of your favorites and ones that you would like to try out. Feel free to substitute protein for protein, fat for fat, focus food for a similar focus food, etc.

For example, if you would like to use chicken instead of beef or avocado oil instead of olive oil, or spinach instead of kale, that is all good.

After you have reviewed the recipe book and highlighted some of the ones that you would like to incorporate, consider some of your own recipes that you would like to also use in your menu plan that you think contain elements of the first two catagories – or could easily be altered so that they DO contain the first two catagories - and add them to your list of possibilities.

Now we will look at the example meals I have provided for you. I have included 20 options for breakfasts, lunch, supper and snack ideas. There are regular meals and "on-the-go" meals, including restaurant meals.

The example meals contain more North American standard meals where you can sub in your favorite recipes for things like roasted chicken, pot roast, taco salad, or protein shakes. If your diet is typically much less standard North American, or vegetarian or vegan, there are some options for you too, although you may need to get a bit more creative with your sub-ins.

Take some time to think about what generally works for your family for meals. Consider the following questions as you begin to build your menu plan:

- What is your current routine?
- Do you need really quick and easy meals in the morning?
- Are there days of the week when you need to work around evening activities?
- Do you eat your lunch out at a restaurant? If so, can you start making your lunch a few days per week, or is there a choice you can make when eating out that follows the three catagories?

- Do you prefer to make extra helpings of supper to have as leftovers the next day?
- Do you have a weekly or monthly special dinner out with your partner, friends, or family?
- Do you have picky eaters who you are trying to accommodate? (And maybe think about if you really need to be accommodating them.)
- What are the standard meals that work for you and your family? Do they contain the three components or do you need to alter them?
- How can you arrange your meals to avoid food spoilage?
- What are your favorite take-out meals? Do they contain the three catagories? If not, are there replacements or a way to alter what you order that you would be happy with and not feel like you are missing out?
- What meals do you like but don't necessarily want to have every week or only enjoy on occasion?
- Do you have a slow cooker or instant pot that you could use to help with meal preparation?
- Is someone else responsible for making the meals, and do they need to be brought in on the planning?

Please take a few minutes to brainstorm out some ideas and some of these things that you need to keep in mind when building your meal plan.

One note for my perfectionist friends – do not aim for perfection. This will not be perfect, and I guarantee you will revise it several times as you go, which is okay. This exercise aims to build something you can work from and change as your or your family's needs and routine change.

Here is my suggestion on how to create a fool-proof meal plan:

First, start by deciding on five days of "regular meals." Remember that this is not a menu plan that needs to be followed precisely. Simply come up with five different breakfasts, five different lunches and five different suppers you will regularly incorporate into your days. This is not a meal plan where you have to eat chicken stir-fry every Wednesday night (unless you want to).

After coming up with five days of regular options, next, decide on five breakfasts, lunches, and suppers that you deem "occasional" meals. These are the meals you may only have once a month or on special occasions. Things that you would like to put in your weekly rotation once or twice per month but not have all the time.

By completing this action step, you will have a full ten days of meal planning to pull from. That is an amazing accomplishment and will really help you move forward as you commit to healthier eating.

The last thing I suggest you do is come up with an additional five days' worth of meals that are all "on the go" meals. Some of these should be quick grab and gos from home, while others should include offerings from your favorite restaurants or takeout. Having five days of "best alternatives" for when you are out and about or unable to cook will help you make the best choices when your choices are limited.

This may take you a couple of hours to complete, so feel free to break it down into smaller chunks. The more time you spend on this and really think about what is realistic for you and your family, the more likely you will be to follow it.

To recap:

1. First, decide on five days of regular meals.
2. Second, come up with five days of "occasional meals" that you will incorporate once or twice a month.
3. Third, come up with five days of on-the-go meals – incorporating both grab-and-go foods and foods you can get from take-out.
4. When you get to chapter 14, you will add your Context Foods to your meal planning

One other consideration to think about is how to avoid food spoilage. Some easy tips for this include buying frozen vegetables and fruit whenever possible and buying a smaller variety of produce at once. For instance, you may eat raw cucumber and broccoli three days in a row and then switch to carrots and cherry tomatoes vs. having a large variety of carrots, cucumbers, peppers, cherry tomatoes, and broccoli all at once. Using one form of greens one week and a different form of greens the following week is another way to avoid everything rotting in your produce drawers.

While having a lot of variety in the diet is important, you don't need to have all the variety all at the same time. In fact, it is a better idea to rotate your foods a bit. You may decide to eat the exact same breakfast for seven days in a row. Great! Then you can switch it up and do something different for another seven days. Remember, the whole point of Context Eating is to give yourself flexibility for what works for you.

CHAPTER 9

MEAL PLANNING FAQ

In this chapter, I want to address common questions and concerns that I receive regarding how to implement the menu plan into your life.

Also, please remember that some of these questions will be covered more fully when we get to section #3 of the Context Eating Method, where we introduce catagory 4. I am asking you to trust the process and stick to the basics, and I promise once you are done reading this book, you will have all the pieces and understand the full Context Eating method more fully.

1. How much food should I be eating in a day?

This is a common question I receive because people are so used to growing up and participating in "diet" plans that have you pre-measure everything you eat and keep you bound to strict measurements of your food.

I do not like that approach because it completely disregards your body's natural rhythms and signals. In fact, one of the main reasons why people overeat is that they no longer listen to their body or the cues to "stop eating."One of the tenets of the Context Eating Method is to help you become more in tune with your body's eating signals. The alternative is a lifetime of measuring and weighing food and relying on outside boundaries to control your eating.

I have given you some guidelines regarding the portions of comfort foods because we have all been conditioned to eat portions that are significantly too large, which can alter blood sugar patterns negatively. This way, if you are still hungry, you can choose to have extra focus or satiating foods that do not impact your blood sugars in the same way that comfort foods can.

2. How many snacks should I be eating every day?

This question goes back to my answer to the first question. If you really need a snack, have a snack. However, over time, and sometimes quite quickly, you will find that you are not hungry between meals and you should drop your snack. If you are going to have a snack, it should still contain, at minimum a focus food and a satiating food. Snacks should never be about grabbing a muffin on your coffee break. More on that later!

3. What about meal spacing or intermittent fasting?

For those who don't know what intermittent fasting is, it is a method in which you limit your eating to a certain time window in the day. Six-hour and eight-hour eating windows are the most common. Intermittent Fasting can be very helpful for some people and not so helpful for others. I personally incorporate IF on a semi-regular basis when it works with my schedule and lifestyle.

The problem with IF is most people are not doing it right. They consume too many refined carbohydrates during their eating window and then fast, which is not helping their blood sugar levels. I also don't think that people with certain conditions should be doing IF all on their own without proper monitoring.

The interesting thing about the Context Eating Method is that you should find that your eating window becomes shorter naturally due to both the satiating foods you are eating and the context you are eating them in. You will also find that your spacing between meals increases, giving your body the ability to reset and regulate blood sugars more efficiently.

That brings us to the next part of the question regarding meal spacing. Again, we want you to start listening for internal cues instead of the time on the clock. Don't force yourself to eat breakfast in the morning if you are not hungry. What is MORE important is what you are starting your day off with.

To lose weight, reduce inflammation, and have more energy, you need to start your day with focus and satiating foods.

Starting with a carbohydrate, even a healthy one, is not something I suggest.

4. What about food intolerances, special diets, and other sensitivities?

There are so many different ways to eat, and different people follow different trains of thought. You could literally eliminate every food available if you tried to follow more than one of these diets at a time. Too many of our clients become overwhelmed when trying to determine the best way to eat. Some claim food intolerances or certain issues like reactions to nightshades or FODMAPS or lectins.

If you are one of these people who is set on eating a certain way, great! You can still use this menu plan and insert whatever alternative foods you think you need. These are not issues we address in this program because we need to start with the basics. If someone thinks their inflammation is caused by nightshade vegetables but has not yet reduced the sugar in their diet, they are getting ahead of themselves.

Yes, food intolerances and even allergies absolutely exist and are something that needs to be looked into if you are in a state of ill health, but they are not the first step. We need first to clean up the diet, support the digestive processes and take steps to balance blood sugar. If, after you have mastered the ideas in this book, you feel that is something you need to look into, please do so.

5. How do you feel about going vegetarian or vegan?

Vegetarianism and veganism are personal choices. I do not subscribe to a diet that is free of animal products. Some people feel great on a plant-based diet, while others can end up feeling quite depleted. There are healthy and unhealthy versions of vegetarianism and veganism. By focusing on focus foods first and then adding satiating foods, many of our clients actually eat more healthy plant-based foods than many vegetarians.

I personally eat a lot of meat, eggs, and fish. If possible, these should be sourced from a high-welfare farm versus a factory farm. Grass-fed and finished meat has a better health profile, and you have a better assurance that the animals are well cared for.

6. What about organic foods?

It is up to you whether or not you choose to buy organic foods. The biggest reason I buy organic foods is to limit the number of pesticides and herbicides I ingest. Good options are any leafy greens, cruciferous vegetables, apples, and berries. Some people are more concerned about some things than others, so do what feels right for you and your family.

7. Where are the treats? How do I incorporate wine and some of my other favorite foods?

I will be showing you how to incorporate your favorite foods, wine, and chocolate in chapter 14. I recommend for the first

106 | DARPAN ALHUWALIA AND KATHY RYAN

two weeks you stick to a more basic eating plan simply because it will force you to think outside of your normal food routine and become aware of some unconscious habits.

Once you learn all about the CONTEXT component of the Context Eating Method, you will understand exactly how to incorporate all other foods that you would like to consume in a healthy way that will eliminate overeating and any feelings of deprivation or guilt. The whole point of the Context Eating Method is that you enjoy your food and eliminate all negative emotional aspects that we attach to food. So hang tight and keep reading!

CHAPTER 10

WHY BLOOD SUGAR BALANCING IS KEY

In this chapter, I will go into a bit more detail about blood sugar and also teach you my way of reading a nutritional label to assess the impact a certain food will have on your blood sugar.

Many of us have dysregulated blood sugar and don't know it. It's not just diabetics or pre-diabetics who have unstable blood sugar. It's a natural outcome of the trappings of our modern North American diet.

As a quick disclaimer, I'm obviously not monitoring your exact blood sugar from moment to moment, so when I talk about blood sugar balancing, what I am really talking about is eating in such a way that is known to help keep blood sugar more stabilized and reduce symptoms of insulin resistance.

First, you need to understand that our diet was very different 150 years ago. There was very little sugar or honey, and "prepared foods" didn't really exist.

The added increase in sugar over the last 150 years has really impacted our insulin response. Insulin is the easiest hormone to directly impact through your food choices. The main role of insulin in the body is to help shuttle glucose into the cells for energy.

When you eat too much sugar or foods high in refined carbohydrates, your body can become resistant to insulin over time. This means the cells begin to ignore the signals from the insulin to take the sugar into the cell.

The best way to explain this is to think of insulin resistance like a line of delivery trucks waiting to unload at a receiving door of a cell. When your cells become insulin resistant, they are closing the receiving gate to the sugar the insulin trucks are trying to unload.

The pancreas will continue to produce more insulin because it is receiving communication that the blood sugar level is still too high. If the pancreas constantly pumps out more insulin, it will eventually get tired and stop working well. This is why so many diabetics need insulin as part of their diabetes management program.

The insulin trucks will continue to back up, trying to get the receiving door of the cell to open. This insulin-resistant condition will inevitably lead to type 2 diabetes, but even before it does, it will cause all kinds of other issues in the body.

When you begin your day with highly refined carbs or sugar, you set yourself up for rollercoaster blood sugar all day long. You go up and then crash and need a quick fix, and then the cycle repeats itself.

Have you ever been HANGRY? This is where your blood sugar dips, and you become literally angry. When you get to this point, you can't wait for your body to digest a steak, so you will naturally gravitate to something like a donut, which will give you quick energy so that you feel better within minutes. The problem with this approach is that very soon, you need another donut because your blood sugar begins dropping again. This is how the negative cycle of craving refined carbohydrates occurs.

Blood sugar dysregulation can lead to:

- Hypoglycemia
- Diabetes
- Polycystic Ovarian Syndrome
- Alzheimer's
- Poor sleep
- Weight gain and inability to lose weight
- A cascade of other hormonal issues
- Increased pain and inflammation
- Increased menopausal symptoms such as hot flashes, night sweats, irritability, and low mood

The thing that you need to remember is sugar is sugar. It all affects your blood sugar levels, and it is one of the biggest contributors to our total stress load on our body. Our body doesn't know the difference between chocolate cupcakes, pure white sugar, pretzels, crackers, or chips. It all impacts your blood sugar. Fruit is also a high source of sugar, although the type of sugar (fructose) is received by the body a bit differently.

I often hear clients saying, "I don't eat very much sugar," but when I review their food journal, I see lots of bread, snacks like chips or pretzels, and other refined carbohydrates that all convert quickly to sugar.

The Context Eating Menu Plan works because it slows down the absorption of food and the conversion to glucose. By ensuring that you are prioritizing focus foods and satiating foods at each meal, you will help slow down this glucose release which can stabilize blood sugar.

Fat, protein, and fiber all lead to feelings of fullness and satiety. This means that you don't eat as much. You fill up more quickly, so you eat less overall. Also, the sugar absorption is slowed down, so you don't get the spike and drops in sugar due to the insulin response.

The way that I have designed the Context Eating Menu Plan has you eating more protein, fat, and fiber vs. refined carbs at any given meal.

Because insulin is the one hormone that is the easiest to control through diet, this is where we need to begin. When any hormone in the body is out of balance, it cascades, throwing many other things out of balance. This is why I can't address issues of hormones or digestion, such as leaky gut, pain and inflammation, weight loss, or even sleep, until I first address this issue with blood sugar.

As you begin to eat in a way that is more conscious of the balance of nutrients, you should begin to see a decrease in cravings and other symptoms, as well as an increase in energy, improved mood, and quality sleep.

One of the ways you can become more conscious of this balance is to learn a simple calculation when you are reading a nutritional label.

I will teach you how I have taught my clients to read a nutrition label from the point of view of blood sugar regulation. This simple calculation can help determine if something may spike your blood sugar or is a more balanced choice. It is a simple calculation that you can do on any labeled food item or any combination of foods you put together to eat at a meal or snack.

This quick, at-a-glance calculation is only from the perspective of the food's probability of spiking your blood sugar. It does not consider any other nutrient markers to determine a food's total nutritional or caloric value.

The calculation indicates total fat plus total protein in grams should be higher than the total carbohydrates minus the total fiber.

Fat+Protein > Carbohydrates - Fiber

Here are two examples of popular snack bars that you can find in a health food store:

Kind Bar - Dark Chocolate Sea Salt

nutrition facts

Serving Size	1 bar (40g)	
	Amount / Serving	% Daily Value
Calories	190	
Total Fat	15g	19%
Saturated Fat	3g	15%
Trans Fat	0g	
Polyunsaturated Fat	3.5g	
Monounsaturated Fat	7g	
Cholesterol	0mg	0%
Sodium	140mg	6%
Total Carbohydrate	16g	6%
Dietary Fiber	7g	25%
Total Sugars	5g	
Includes 4g Added Sugars		4%
Sugar Alcohol	0g	
Protein	6g	
Vitamin D		0%
Calcium		4%
Iron		6%
Potassium		4%

Using the above calculation, you take the total fat 15 and add it to the total protein 6 to get 21.

Then you take the total carbohydrates minus the total fiber, which is 16-7 = 9

Therefore, the total amount of fat+protein (21) is GREATER than the total amount of carbohydrates - fiber (9), so from a blood sugar influencing perspective, this bar is a good choice.

Cliff Bar - Chocolate Chip

Nutrition Facts	Amount/serving	% DV	Amount/serving	% DV	Amount/serving	% DV
Serv. size 1 bar (68g)	Total Fat 6g	8%	Sodium 130mg	6%	Total Sugars 17g	
	Sat. Fat 2g	9%	Total Carb. 43g	16%	Incl. 16g Added Sugars	32%
	Trans Fat 0g		Dietary Fiber 5g	19%	Protein 10g	19%
Calories per serving **250**	Cholesterol 0mg	0%				
	Vit. D 0mcg 0% • Calcium 45mg 4% • Iron 2mg 10% • Potas. 256mg 6% • Vit. E 5% • Phosphorus 15% • Magnesium 15%					

In this second example, you take the total fat 6 + the total protein 10, which equals 16.

Then you take the total carbohydrates 43 and minus the fiber 5 to get 38.

Therefore the total fat + protein (16) is LESS THAN the total carbohydrates - fiber (38), so from a blood sugar influencing perspective, this is not the best choice.

You can easily do this with any packaged food with a nutritional label.

Take some time to go through your pantry and fridge to get an idea about some of the things you regularly consume. You can even look up some of your favorite take-out foods online. You may be surprised about how many "healthy" packaged foods you are eating that may be negatively impacting your blood sugars.

One note of caution. As I mentioned, this calculation does not measure anything else about the nutritional value of the food you are looking at. You may have a very high-fat food with all kinds of additives and preservatives that meet the criteria for keeping your blood sugars in check. It doesn't mean that the food is healthy; it simply means that it has less of a chance of dysregulating your blood sugars.

Remember, whenever you have higher fat, higher protein, or higher fiber, the absorption of your carbohydrates will be slowed down, which may lead to more balanced blood sugar. Having wine with some cheese or having wine with your meal is better from a blood sugar-balancing perspective than having wine on its own. Having a small portion of pasta with a heavier meat sauce and cheese is better from a blood sugar-balancing perspective than having a larger plate of pasta with a simple low-fiber vegetarian tomato sauce.

Keeping these things in mind when you are learning to Context Eat can help keep you feeling satiated and lower the impact of dysregulated blood sugar on your ability to lose weight.

PART III

CONTEXT

CHAPTER 11

THE SECRET SAUCE

This is the section you've been waiting for. This is where I break down the "secret sauce" of the Context Eating Method and why it works so well for many people stuck in all-or-nothing approaches and yo-yo dieting. This is where I help you navigate the best ways to incorporate all your favorite foods into your life in a way that is healthier, contained, and free from feelings of deprivation on one end or guilt on the other end.

The problem with dieting is that there is no sustainable way to incorporate what I call your Context Foods. As mentioned previously, Context Foods are the foods that you enjoy for the experience. They are the foods you celebrate, treat yourself with, or indulge in. They are often high in sugar or contain little to no nutrient value. They may be very high in calories or have a combination of ingredients that are not conducive to health. Or, they may just be something you need to set some boundaries around. I call them Context Foods because these foods should ideally only be eaten in certain contexts.

With most diets, these types of foods are either completely restricted, or you are told you can have them "in moderation." "In moderation" is a term that we hear all the time, but what exactly does it mean?

A few years ago, the 80-20 rule was being promoted. If you ate well 80% of the time, then the other 20% of less healthy food won't impact you as much. While I understand the intention of this idea, and I've even used it occasionally when I am offering quick answers or advice where a more lengthy explanation is not warranted, it is not entirely true.

First, how do you determine your 80-20% ratio? Secondly, who says the 20% is not actually a problem? Thirdly, it contains this same morality-based idea that I will "behave" 80% of the time and "be bad" 20% of the time.

"In moderation" doesn't really mean anything, and there are no real defined parameters of "in moderation." Is eating a tub of Ben and Jerry's in one sitting once a week "in moderation?" Maybe…and then you also "drink wine two times per week in moderation," and then eat chips "in moderation," and then drink your sweetened iced coffee "in moderation?"

This is what happens when you focus on the FOOD. Some targets and boundaries tend to move around because there are no defined parameters for eating a specific food. Context Eating takes away a lot of this ambiguity and gives you healthier boundaries in which to enjoy your Context Foods.

The goal of the first step of the Context Eating Method was to get you to become aware of overeating triggers and unconscious habits that were leading to your weight gain.

The second step was to prioritize your hydration, build a menu plan containing focus and satiating foods, and identify proper portions of comfort foods.

The third step of the Context Eating Method is to help you achieve long-term health and weight loss without an all-or-nothing approach. This is what this next section is all about.

You may wonder why I waited so late in the book to fully introduce the "Context" part of the Context Eating Method. This is because I needed you first to understand the root causes of what may be contributing to your weight gain or inability to release and keep weight off and set the stage for some foundational awareness and change in habits.

If I jumped right into the Context Eating approach, you would not fully understand your own context. Your context is everything about YOU, and I will explain that in better detail in these next couple of chapters.

The Context Eating Method is all about an alternative way of approaching food that will allow those who have experienced a disordered relationship with food or who have a long history of yo-yo dieting to find the proper context to reincorporate their favorite foods without having to try to implement an all-or-nothing approach.

Every diet that currently exists, with the possible exception of intermittent fasting, is focused primarily on WHAT you are eating.

This one-dimensional approach has been used in countless programs where followers are simply instructed to change what they are eating. These programs break down food into categories that recognize them as either good" or "bad" food. They may not actually use these terms, but the message comes through clearly when there is talk of permitted foods vs. restricted foods or an unlimited food list vs. a limited food list.

Terms like nutrient dense/nutrient void or high calorie/low calorie create a hierarchy where the goal of the program is to choose more good food and less bad food.

While this is a reasonable approach to assess things like nutrient density, as I have done with the four-catagory menu plan, it does not take into account what I believe to be the more important metrics of our food choices.

In the past few years, the cliché "it's not a diet, it's a lifestyle" has also been thrown around as a solution to counter the idea of quick-fix or fad diets. While this sounds good in theory, the distinction between the two is quite vague. Most "lifestyle" programs are simply permanent diets dressed up in more health-friendly language. If you are making a choice to change your lifestyle that completely removes certain foods from your life…it's a diet…just a permanent one.

This simplistic approach of trying to help someone change "what" they eat will almost always fail because it does not consider the full scope of the issues surrounding people who struggle with disordered eating. It forces them into life-long restrictions that require an ongoing high level of discipline that can result in feelings of deprivation.

The interesting thing about this "simplistic approach" is that it is, at the same time, incredibly complex. The list of dos and don'ts, managing calculations of macros or calories, weighing food, or adhering to certain food-combining principles and strict menu plans can be an all-encompassing effort that most busy, stressed-out people don't have the time to manage or maintain. This complexity causes individuals to quickly abandon their goals and wait until the next new program makes its rounds.

If we want to see people succeed in getting to and maintaining healthy body composition, we need to turn this whole idea on its head. We need to stop treating food as a friend or enemy. Treating food as either good or bad takes disordered eating to a whole new level of struggle. It is no longer just a physical or emotional struggle; it becomes a moral struggle.

If you eat bad food, you have done something bad; therefore, you must be a bad or undisciplined person. This self-abasing mindset further complicates our already emotionally-driven responses to food and creates "moral" dilemmas and designations where none should exist.

What is needed is an approach that takes away the idea that food is a moral choice. We need to move the attention away from planning, calculating, and restricting to a more holistic, intuitive, and affirming approach.

However, the problem I have found with the intuitive eating movement is that it is not structured enough for most people. Context Eating is the intersection between body positivity, intuitive eating, and a structured diet.

The best-case scenario would be to introduce a method that allows people autonomy over WHAT they eat and place the focus on other situational parameters.

The premise of Context Eating is that the context the food is consumed in is more important than the food itself. With the Context Eating Method, I teach that no food is off limits within its proper context and instead teach other parameters that can be used to make balanced food choices to assist you in meeting your health and body composition goals. This method of eating can be used in conjunction with any other program an individual chooses to participate in.

The context approach to eating goes beyond WHAT you are eating and asks more important questions about your food situation. Instead of asking, "What are you eating?" the Context Method asks much more interesting questions. Questions like who, when, where, and why.

In the next chapter, I discuss how these questions can completely change your approach to food and how incorporating the context method of eating can promote health and well-being on a much deeper level than simply a restrictive diet.

CHAPTER 12

ASKING YOURSELF THE RIGHT QUESTIONS

In this chapter, I will discuss the parameters of the context eating method. The parameters are who, what, when, where, and why.

1. WHO

There are two parts to the question WHO. The first is, WHO are you? Who is eating? Who you are currently will directly affect your current eating decisions and habits.

Factors that influence the way that you eat include:

- Your age
- Your stage of life
- Your history
- Your ethnicity/traditions
- Your current health – physical/emotional

- Your current stress levels and life situation
- Your finances
- Your personality and personal preferences

This may sound simplistic, and it is, but sometimes we miss the most obvious things.

Are you a 17-year-old star track athlete or a perimenopausal woman with hormone imbalance, dysregulated blood sugars, and a family history of heart disease?

Are you a postpartum breastfeeding mom or a sedentary office administrator in your fifties?

Are you an eight-year-old child or a twenty-three-year-old young adult?

Are you an active floor manager who walks 20,000 steps during their working hours, or are you currently recovering from knee surgery?

I often hear women say, "I don't know why I am gaining weight because I still eat the way I did when I was in my 20s, and I was so skinny then." Yes, this is precisely why you are gaining weight, because you are eating the same way you did when you had a very different body. Remember, your body completely replaces itself every seven years or so, so you are literally not the same person you were when you were 20.

Oftentimes I will have clients quoting advice they have heard from health and fitness influencers who have an audience with a completely different demographic than they. What a 20-year-old bodybuilder needs will be different than what a 45-year-old perimenopausal mother of three needs.

Who you are matters. Who you personally are should have a lot of bearing on what you choose to eat.

After figuring out who you are, the second part of the WHO question is WHO are you eating with? This question does not require a lot of thought as it should be fairly obvious who you share space with while you eat.

- Alone
- Spouse/Partner
- Children
- Extended family
- Friends
- Co-workers
- Clients or Business Associates
- Acquaintances or Strangers
- Alone but with Strangers (ie, in a restaurant)

You might not consciously realize how much WHO you are eating with influences your eating choices within a given situation. Take a moment to think about the above groupings and how differently you eat depending upon who you are with.

Each group has specific traditions and culturally accepted norms that will greatly influence food choices and routines. Some of these situations will encourage you to make healthier choices, while others will discourage that practice. Identifying the particular "eating realities" within these groups will help you better respond to each situation.

For instance, are there traditions around coffee or lunch breaks that impede your ability to make the best choices at work? Does someone bring in donuts every day? Are birthdays celebrated with cake in the lunchroom? Does your group go out for lunch daily? Weekly?

Do you and your spouse have a weekly date night or pizza night with the family?

Do get-togethers with your extended family revolve around a lot of food?

Do you regularly wine and dine with friends or business associates?

Do you go to a bar to watch the game and load up on beer and nachos?

Do you live and eat alone where your food consumption is free from any stipulations or outward judgment?

What is the health and lifestyle of those whom you spend the most time with?

Each of these scenarios greatly impacts your food choices. For instance, you will probably not choose to eat a whole container of Ben and Jerry's while at a fancy dinner with a client or indulge in too much wine while sitting in the office lunchroom on a coffee break.

Understanding these context norms allows you to see how certain situations create natural barriers to eating one type or amount of food, while other situations may create barriers to eating another type or amount of food. Context Eating aims to take full advantage of these natural barriers while also understanding the liabilities that exist within certain contexts.

Thinking about who you are and who you are with is the first step within the Context Eating Method. Don't worry about what this means and how to apply it yet. I will first go through all the different context parameters and then put them together in the next chapter.

2. WHAT

As previously stated, the "what" you are eating is typically the first thing people look at when trying to change health and diet. This is the first area we as a society try to exercise control over, often eliminating full food groups or categorizing food within two categories of "bad" and "good."

Categorizing food as either "bad" or "good" has many emotional and psychological implications for someone with disordered eating. Phrases such as "I cheated today" or "I was bad today" are very common and are either said by my clients with a child-like, gleeful rebellion or complete failure and despair. Both these scenarios are not helpful as the individual becomes their rebellion or failure. If you are an emotional eater, this morality-based eating results in more disordered eating. In fact, I believe this morality-based eating is causing the vast majority of the problems we see with emotional-based disordered eating.

When someone has been told that they "shouldn't be eating" a particular amount or type of food, that often becomes the first thing they want to do, especially if they have been shamed for eating a certain way. Many of my clients will recount how their eating is often commented on or judged by a family member, friend, or sometimes even a stranger. This then becomes the point where certain eating habits become hidden and occur when nobody is around. The contexts in which it is healthier for them to be eating a lot of food (i.e., at a party or celebration with lots of people) become the contexts where they eat very little to avoid judgment, but then they go home, and binge eat what they actually wanted to be eating.

This is precisely what I am trying to avoid with Context Eating. From the point of context, it is much healthier for you to completely enjoy your food choices in the presence of family and friends versus overeating when you are alone.

All that said, "what" you are eating is obviously an important part of the health equation, but questions around what you are eating should include nutrient density, caloric density, inflammatory response, and individual requirements, not whether a food is "good" or "bad." This is what the 3 catagory approach you are currently using focuses on.

Nutrient density: If you have been in the diet game for some time, you will know the basic premise of what constitutes nutrient dense vs. nutrient-void food. You know eating more vegetables and less baked goods is good for your waistline and health, but often the reason you are given is only in regards to the number of calories the food contains. A food is considered "good" if it contains fewer calories and "bad" if it contains more calories. This logic has led people to believe that a 100-calorie snack bar is a better choice than an avocado.

If the number of calories is the sole measure of a priority food group, then all those eating the 100-calorie snack bars and low-fat yogurts should have perfect health and body composition, which is just not the case. Your body uses broccoli differently than it uses a low-fat ice cream bar.

Caloric density: On the flip side, calories may be important for you to be aware of, but only within a particular context. If you are active, you will require more calories than if you are not active. Having a general idea of how many calories you should be consuming a day is not a bad idea (do you use 1500 calories per day or 3000 calories per day?), but getting caught up on counting every single calorie doesn't do anyone any good. Portion awareness is an important step on your health journey, but having to weigh and measure everything takes away the enjoyment and experience of your food.

Inflammatory response: The next thing you should consider is how you feel when you eat a certain food. Does it cause an increase in your pain, brain fog, or digestive upset? Does it cause issues with blood sugar regulation? Does it negatively impact your energy or sleep? Knowing how your body responds to certain foods will help you more naturally avoid foods that cause you pain or discomfort.

Understanding the "what" of food is important information and needs to go beyond "how many calories" it contains. Once again, if this is all we are looking at, we are missing the most important factors in determining what someone should eat and how they can incorporate some of their favorite foods.

Let's take the example of a piece of cake.

Cake belongs within the category four, Context Food section of the menu plan. It is full of sugar, oils, and additives. It has very little nutrient value and a high caloric value. When it comes to the diet world, cake is a "bad" food. When you decide to "go on a diet," you automatically understand that cake will not be on your menu plan.

You know that if you eat cake while you are on your diet, you are either "off plan" or "cheating." This means you are not "sticking to" your diet. Think of what that does to you from a psychological perspective. If you eat the cake, you are failing at your diet. If you eat the cake and you fail at your diet, you might as well go ahead and have three pieces of cake, ice cream, and half a bottle of wine because you've already failed. Then, maybe you can correct course and start "being good" again the following Monday.

Whether you will cheat or not on your diet when you eat a piece of cake quickly leads to morality-based food choices.

The WHAT is important to a point, but making it the sole determining factor is something that we need to get away from to move into a less restrictive and more holistic way of eating.

That is why when you eat cake on the Context Eating menu plan, you are still on plan. There is no cheating. You are fully empowered to make the decision to eat cake, and I will show you exactly how to do that in the next chapter.

3. WHEN

When are you eating?

Eating the exact same food at different times can produce different outcomes. There are better and worse times to be eating certain foods.

For instance, if you eat a high amount of carbs first thing in the morning, you are more likely to crave carbs all day and eat in a way that promotes dysregulated blood sugar.

Eating too many times throughout the day can also negatively impact your blood sugar and ability to lose weight.

What you eat before and after your workout can impact the workout's effectiveness.

Eating because it's "time to eat" vs. waiting until you are actually hungry can contribute to disordered eating, where you stop depending on your natural hunger cues to tell you it's time to eat.

Other considerations for WHEN you eat include eating seasonally.

Eating fruits and vegetables that are in season will help with nutrient density, taste, and enjoyment. Eat from your garden as much as possible.

For seasonal treats, homemade Christmas baking in the month of December, strawberry shortcake in the middle of June, corn on the cob with mounds of butter and salt at a corn roast in August, and an ice cream cone in the middle of the summer as a family outing are all examples of seasonal treats.

Seasonal eating may also include tuning into the natural and seasonal rhythms of the body. Historically, people traditionally ate more in the warmer months, less over the winter, and into the spring.

Something else that you may want to consider when looking at WHEN to eat is fasting or intermittent fasting. Intermittent fasting, when done properly, is a great way to place healthy "WHEN" parameters around your eating. It is beyond the scope of this book to dive into the do's and don'ts of intermittent fasting, but suffice it to say that it is a tool that can be very helpful in releasing and keeping off unhealthy weight.

As previously mentioned, learning to Context Eat will naturally reduce your "eating window," giving you many of the same benefits that intermittent fasting can give you without learning how to incorporate IF properly.

4. WHERE

This factor and the last one, "why," are the two biggest factors contributing to poor eating habits. If we could improve these

DARPAN ALHUWALIA AND KATHY RYAN | 133

context eating parameters, we could transform the body composition and eating habits of almost everybody.

When you think of some of the most common places that people eat, the following places come to mind:

- The car/the bus/the train/ the plane
- Arena/at kids' activities
- The couch
- The theater
- Standing at the kitchen counter
- At your desk
- In bed
- At a restaurant or party
- Sit-down dinner with family
- Outside

The bathroom is pretty much the only place where (most) people don't eat.

The vast majority of these places that you eat are places where you are also doing something else.

If you are in the car or bus, you travel and sometimes even drive. If you are sitting on the couch or on your bed, you are probably watching TV or staring at your phone. If you are eating at your desk, you are probably working. If you are standing at the kitchen counter, you might be cooking or simply rushing through your meal to get onto the next thing.

Distracted eating is one of the biggest reasons you eat too much or don't feel satiated after eating. Eating should be a multisensory process, but if you are eating while doing anything else, you do not have the full attention of your senses on your food.

This goes back to the ideas of "Downton Abbey" and the upleveling of your food experience. You do yourself and your food a disservice by treating the action of eating a meal in a careless or flippant manner. When you stop and think about everything that had to happen for that food to end up on your plate, you begin to slow down and truly appreciate the miracle that it is.

If you sat down at a table, ate your meal, left the table, and did not eat again until you returned to a table, you would naturally begin to release unwanted weight.

Think about how you eat when you sit down at a table vs. how you eat when you are not at a table. When not at a table, you choose easy foods. Finger foods, fast foods, cookies, crackers, muffins, french fries, simple sandwiches, fruit, smoothies, and more. You "graze," nibble, or search the cupboard or fridge for something easy. Things like a spoonful of ice cream, peanut butter, or a handful of chips.

At the table, you have a fork, knife, and spoon. You have a plate and a glass for your water. You tend to eat more slowly and deliberately. If you are with other people, you may be having a conversation during your meal, which further slows down the eating process.

One of the biggest differences in how we ate in the 1940s vs. now is that everyone sat down at a table to eat. We didn't have to-go foods in the way that we do now. We didn't eat in the car on the way to practice or while sitting at our desks. We didn't down a smoothie after a workout. We didn't have options for 500-calorie snacks. We didn't have Netflix marathons with the addition of every movie snack possible. There was no food available on every street corner, and sugar was an occasional addition to our day, not something contained in every piece of food that we ate.

Think about this. If all you ate was three meals a day, even if all three of your meals were 500 calories, which is a decent-sized home-cooked meal, you would only be eating 1500 calories per day. Not because you were counting calories but because you were limiting your eating to the context of sitting at a table.

5. WHY

We eat for many more reasons than just stopping hunger pain...

Why are you eating? Are you actually hungry, or...

- Are you bored?
- Are you distracted?
- Are you satisfying a craving?
- Was it just "there?"
- Are you tired?
- Are you sad?
- Are you lonely?
- Are you celebrating?
- Are you feeling obligated?
- Are you afraid?
- Or...Is your body protecting you from something?

Becoming aware of WHY you are eating and choosing to limit the context of your eating to when you are hungry is the other most impactful thing that you can do to eliminate overeating and get you back in sync with your body's natural rhythms.

This can take some intentionality, but this is where combining healthier contexts like where you are eating and when you are eating can be so powerful.

Becoming aware of your eating when you are bored or sad or because the food "was there" is one of the best things you can do to stop overeating or eating within less healthy contexts. The goal isn't to completely eliminate emotional eating from your life because, let's be real, when you are in a certain state, you probably don't care that you are emotionally eating. The goal is to reduce the triggers that lead to emotional eating and to stop the continuous pattern of emotional eating so that it becomes an infrequent event in your life.

So those are the five areas of consideration when it comes to Context Eating. Now I want to teach you what these considerations look like in your day-to-day life and how to apply catagory four, Context, to your meals.

CHAPTER 13

PRACTICE MAKES PERFECT

Now that you have had an introduction to the who, what, when, where, and why of Context Eating, we now need to discuss how this simple understanding can completely change how you make your food choices.

In this chapter, we look at different scenarios where the context of the food, rather than the food itself, becomes the bigger consideration in whether the food you eat is a good choice.

The first thing that we need to ask is: Why is this process important?

It's important because it takes the focus off the "what" and puts food back into proper context. It takes away guilt and deprivation and empowers you to make food choices based on CONTEXT rather than the food itself.

Some examples help further demonstrate how the food is the same, but the eating contexts are very different.

Having a glass of wine (what) at a dinner party (where) with friends (who) may be a healthy context for drinking alcohol. However, if you are an alcoholic (who) or you are drinking alone because you are sad (why), it may not be a healthy context.

Enjoying an ice cream cone (what) at Dairy Queen (where) with your family (who) in the summer (when) may be a healthy context for enjoying some ice cream. Having a pint of Häagen-Dazs (what) in the middle of January (when) when you are at home sick with a bad cold (who) may not be the best context.

Eating a big plate of raw vegetables, including tomatoes and peppers (what), may be a healthy context for a snack, but if you are someone who has an inflammatory response to nightshade vegetables (who), it may not be the best context.

Eating chocolate cake (what) at your child's birthday party (why/where) surrounded by friends and family (who) may be a good, healthy context for chocolate cake. Eating leftover chocolate (what) cake at 3 a.m (when), alone (who) in the kitchen (where) "because it was there" (why) may not be a healthy food context.

Eating a couple of pieces of homemade Christmas baking at a Christmas party may be a good, healthy context for eating sweets. Eating a donut daily in the lunch room because someone keeps bringing them in and you "don't want them to go to waste" may not be the best context for eating sweets.

Drinking a soda at a party as a healthy young adult may be a good context for drinking a soda. Drinking a soda when you are four years old may not be the best context for drinking a soda.

Eating 500 calories at a sit-down meal with your family may be a healthy context for eating 500 calories. Eating a 500-calorie snack in the car as you drive your child to their hockey game may not be a healthy context.

Enjoying a couple of slices of pizza with your family on family pizza night may be a healthy context for eating pizza. Eating leftover pizza as a snack (while you are bored and sitting and watching TV when you aren't hungry and are not even enjoying it because it is a bit stale) may not be the healthiest context.

Drinking a raw green smoothie every day may be healthy, but drinking a raw green smoothie every day with little to no other balance of nutrients by a person with an eating disorder may not be the healthiest context.

The same food with completely different contexts leads to different food outcomes.

Let's go back to the example of the cake.

Typically, when someone with disordered eating finishes a large piece of chocolate cake at 11 p.m. because it was there, there is a response of regret, maybe even disgust, and possibly a vow never to eat chocolate cake again!

This individual is solely focused on the "WHAT," the chocolate cake. The chocolate cake is the problem they are focused on at that moment. It's BAD food. Not the fact that it is 11 pm, and they should have gone to bed. Not the fact that they are alone.

Not the fact that they are tired. Not the fact that it is an unhealthy context for eating chocolate cake.

When the sole focus becomes the problem of the chocolate cake, the vow never to eat the problem food again will often surface.

But, here is the thing. They will eat chocolate cake again because they don't have control over their triggers. They do not recognize their triggers because they are still focused on the fact that the chocolate cake is the problem.

But chocolate cake is not the problem; the context is the problem.

I hope this makes sense.

What if, instead of having all kinds of negative feelings towards the cake and blaming the cake for their weight gain and their overindulging, they step back and evaluate the eating context:

They notice that when they stay up too late or are tired, sad, or overwhelmed, they are more likely to eat something just "because it was there."

They recognize that having leftover cake in the house is not a good idea, so they make a decision to set a boundary not to have leftover chocolate cake in the house.

They still allow themselves to eat the chocolate cake in a healthier context, like a family birthday party, avoiding the "this is the last time I will ever eat cake, so I'm going to overindulge right now" scenario.

I started doing this in my own family.I only buy or make a small birthday cake, so everyone gets one piece. Before this decision, my eating one piece of cake at a party turned into eating four pieces of cake over the next couple of days simply because it was there. So now, no leftovers come home. I enjoy my one piece of cake and wait for the next birthday party to enjoy another piece of cake. I don't worry about saving points or counting calories or macros. I don't feel any guilt for eating cake at a birthday party. For me, when it comes to the context of a birthday party, cake is a healthy choice.

As an aside, I will often hear clients say they eat the cake or other leftovers so that "it doesn't go to waste." So just a reminder for those who need to hear it: you are not a human garburator – THROW IT OUT!

Eating within healthy contexts is also something you can teach your children because it provides natural boundaries to certain foods. Unfortunately, most toddlers are learning that food belongs in all contexts. They eat in the car, in the park, in front of the TV, while playing with their toys, while waiting, and while needing to be entertained.

Parents have embraced the idea that toddlers tend to "graze" more than eat proper meals. We are teaching our toddlers that food is everywhere and can and should be eaten at any time. They then carry this idea that food belongs everywhere into their teen and adult years.

Teaching your children good and bad food "contexts" rather than good and bad foods further encourages healthy habits as they move into adulthood.

Instead of saying things like, "that food is bad for you," you can say things like, "oh yes, that food is yummy, and we will have some [within a specific context] on Friday night during our family movie night."

As a kid, I had a Friday night (homemade) pizza night, and Saturday morning, I was allowed sugary cereal. I could drink Kool-Aid when we were at the cottage. Fast food was reserved for birthday parties, as was chocolate cake. Dessert came after Sunday dinner when we had guests over. There were no cookie clubs at the grocery store or lollipops after a haircut. I only got candy at Halloween and in birthday party loot bags.

Were all these choices healthy from a nutritional standpoint? Absolutely not. Were all of these contexts good eating contexts? Probably not, as personally, I don't think there is any context where kids should be drinking Kool-Aid. The point is, I knew there was no point in asking for sugary cereal on a Wednesday morning. We were never going to have McDonald's on a random Tuesday night.It was never going to happen. There was a firm boundary there.

It's not that McDonald's, chocolate cake, and pop didn't exist when I was growing up; it's that it was kept within its proper context.

As adults, we can do the same thing: apply some strict eating context boundaries to help put food back in its proper context.

The other area we need to think about is "Why are we eating?"

Consider the reasons people give as to why they ate something. Out of these twelve reasons to eat something, only one and possibly one other are actually valid reasons to be eating:

- Hunger
- Bored
- Distracted
- Satisfying a craving
- It was "there"
- Tired
- Sad
- Lonely
- Celebrating/happy
- Obligated/ Social Construct
- Afraid
- The body is protecting you from some "threat."

If you could eliminate the other ten reasons you are eating by acknowledging that they are not valid contexts, you could completely change your relationship with food, your body composition, and your health.

Context is everything. This approach teaches that no food is off limits within its proper context and instead teaches parameters that can be used to make balanced food choices.

Eating within context eliminates the "good" and "bad" foods to eat and instead emphasizes an awareness of unconscious patterns, triggers, and negative habits that promote disordered eating, weight gain, and poor health. It's a completely individualized approach and promotes self-regulation, awareness, and the ability to adapt to certain situations and stages of life.

CHAPTER 14

BEST PRACTICES FOR INTEGRATING CONTEXT EATING INTO YOUR LIFE

Before we finish off talking about context, there are a couple of caveats, cautions, and best practices that I need to communicate to ensure that the ideas behind Context Eating are not misused.

What I don't want you to do is use your current lifestyle as an excuse to continue eating all the time in less optimum contexts. For example, if you say, "We have hockey every night, so we have to eat in the car every night," I will challenge you on that. This process may reveal other areas of life that need to come back into balance. If life activities lead to disordered eating and continuous less healthy food contexts, then it may be time to make other changes.

Throughout my years coaching people in nutrition, I am always amazed at the number of grown, adult women who have very child-like responses to food. I have already mentioned the gleeful rebellion I see when someone tells me they "cheated," but it often goes further than that. Many women who say, "Just tell me what to do," are actually asking me to parent them.

They want ME (an "authority" in their life) to tell them when they can and can't eat. They want me to decide their boundaries for them. This is not a good or healthy approach. Not only are they giving their autonomy away, but there is also a greater chance of a negative emotional response (gleeful rebellion or complete despair) when they "go off plan" and "let down" the authority who is making the rules for them.

Only you can determine your non-negotiables and the things you are willing to let go of. If pizza night with the family is a non-negotiable, then maybe you need to start by eliminating your daily Starbucks or at least changing your order.

It's not the thing that you are doing once in a while that is drastically impacting your health; it's the things you do every day. If you are constantly justifying disordered eating because you are "busy/stressed/celebrating/ treating yourself," that is not the point of this exercise. The point is to become mindful of what you are eating, why you are eating, when you are eating, where you are eating, and who you are eating with so that you can make choices from a place of empowerment that don't require completely eliminating your enjoyment of food. In fact, the reverse will happen. You will enjoy your food choices so much more because of their special meaning within the context you are eating them, and there will be no associated guilt.

Prioritize your favorite Context foods. Exercise the idea of "fasting and feasting." Going without your daily Starbucks will allow you to enjoy family pizza night guilt-free. Eating pizza during family pizza night is a decision you are making versus a default setting. There is power in making a food-related decision. There is no power in going with the flow because it is a default setting. Making an empowered decision renders the emotional and morality-based responses to food powerless.

As an informal action step, ask yourself how often you make morality-based food choices or use words like "good, bad, cheat, binge, treating myself, etc." when you refer to the food you eat or yourself based on the food choices you have made.

Think about how this thinking affects your relationship with food and yourself. What are the stories you tell yourself about yourself every time you eat a food that you enjoy that is not very nutrient dense? One of the main points of Context Eating is to break the power of the negative emotions that you have attached to eating certain foods.

Here are some other best practices you can begin to incorporate immediately to help you make Context Eating work for you.

1. Combine your Context Foods with Focus Foods and Satiating Foods. If you are going to a birthday party and have pizza and birthday cake, always add some focus foods or satiating foods to your meal. Incorporate a salad with your pizza. Order some (non-breaded) wings to add to the satiating component and eat higher protein, higher fat foods first before you eat your pizza. One of the things I do all the time now is take some inulin or acacia fiber before I have something like pizza. When you do this, you will find that you naturally reduce the amount of Context Foods you eat because you are already satiated.

2. Limit all your eating to the context of a table with no distractions (i.e.screens/work). As previously mentioned, this one context will help you put food back in its proper place in your life. That means no eating in the car, at the kitchen counter, at your desk, on the couch, in bed, or in front of the TV. Table only.

What you will find with this "table only" approach is that a lot of the food that was previously fun to eat is no longer that interesting. What I mean by that is: WHERE do you usually eat a whole bag of cookies or chips or an extra large chocolate bar, or where do you drink a 600-calorie white chocolate mocha frappuccino? These are not typically "table" foods.

These are car foods, desk foods, or in front of the TV foods. When clients begin working with me, I tell them they can eat whatever they want, but they need to sit at a table with no distractions. They initially think it is amazing that I am permitting them to eat whatever they want, but they very quickly realize that eating most of those foods at a table doesn't feel right.

It actually feels weird to sit down at a table and focus on drinking an iced coffee or eating a chocolate bar. It's a weird context for this type of food. When I first started applying the table-only rule to my own life, I found that when I went grocery shopping, I suddenly didn't want to buy chips or even protein bars because I wasn't interested in sitting down at my table to eat these things.

And this brings up the main reason WHY context eating works. We are breaking the addictive situational contexts. "When I watch a movie, I eat pizza and popcorn." "When I drive to work, I eat a chocolate chip muffin." "When I sit at my desk and concentrate on my work, I eat chocolate." "When I have a moment to myself to scroll my phone, I sit on the couch and have a snack."

Bringing food back to the context of the table is the biggest concrete boundary that you can place on your eating that requires zero discipline about WHAT you are eating.

This process has you stopping the idea of "I can't eat this food" and instead says, "I can eat this food, but only at the table." Then you get to decide whether you would rather sit at the table and eat your chips or watch your favorite TV show.

When you begin this approach, you will catch yourself eating at places that are not a table all day long. You will become aware of how much you are eating as you make your meal or how often you grab something out of the cupboard to munch on as you go about your day. You may begin to recognize how much food you eat while driving or sitting in bed.

Initially, all you need to do when you become aware of what you are eating is go and sit at a table. You will quickly learn how boring that is, even if you are eating something you usually enjoy. The fact is, changing the context back to the table will cause you to enjoy fast food much less.

What this also does is limit your eating window. Instead of your eating window being dragged out from when you start cooking dinner to when you turn off the lights to go to bed, you will be limited in your eating to the time you spend at the table, which is likely a half hour to an hour. This alone will improve your insulin response and blood sugar levels.

This is also where you want to add your favorite foods. If you want to have something sweet or a glass of wine, have it sitting at a table with your regular meal that incorporates the other 2 or 3 catagories of focus foods, satiating foods, and comfort foods.

3. Give thanks for your food before you consume it. In many traditions, there is an act of giving thanks or saying grace before you consume your meal. This often becomes a rote, superficial act and doesn't hold the significance that it should. When you are giving thanks for your meal, think about all that had to happen to get your food to your plate. Taking even a few seconds to contemplate this is another small way to help uplevel your food experience.

4. Incorporate as many focus foods as you can. I can't stress this enough. Especially fermented foods like sauerkraut and apple cider vinegar. These have incredibly positive benefits on your microbiome, which changes the whole way your body assimilates your food. Add some sauerkraut with your bacon and eggs. Put a teaspoon of apple cider vinegar in your smoothie. One of the easiest things that you can do is have a small glass of water with a teaspoon of apple cider vinegar, freshly squeezed lemon, and a ¼ teaspoon of moringa powder or some other nutrient-dense green powder. Even adding this to a meal that is not the most nutrient-dense will help tremendously and start opening doors to better health over time.

5. Sweets are desserts, not snacks. Too many of our snacks are sugary. Whether it's a muffin, granola bar, bowl of cereal, or a decadent iced coffee, these things should be considered desserts, not snacks. If you decide to eat these things, eat them as desserts after your meal. Then, as you continue in this Context Eating process, you can begin asking yourself if you even need to have dessert every day, or is this a habit you are now ready to drop?

6. Make it a habit to evaluate your eating context continuously. Ask yourself: "What is my eating context?" Go through who, what, when, where, and why quickly in your head. It would be great if, every time you were eating something in a less than optimal food context (like a bag of chips alone in front of the TV because you're bored), you were able to interrupt the pattern and decide NOT to eat the bag of chips but just to go and enjoy watching your show, yet that is not always going to happen. Sometimes you will acknowledge the bad context and go ahead and eat it anyway. Obviously, the goal is to have these bad food contexts decrease over time, and the sooner you master that, the sooner you will achieve your health goals. However, the whole point is that it is a learning process where you start to become aware of your habits, address those triggers, and begin to interrupt the pattern.

Even something as simple as the pattern of going through the drive-through can be changed to a different context. Ask yourself if you really need to eat the food in the car on the way home, or can you wait until you get home and sit at the table? You may decide that you don't want to wait until you get home to eat the food because it will be cold by then, so you opt not to get take-out at all.

The point is to question your eating context rather than just doing it automatically.

- WHO am I eating with? I am alone.
- WHAT am I eating? A triple cheeseburger and large fries. Hmm, could I make a different choice?
- When am I eating? At 11 p.m. on my way home from a friend's house. Hmm, that's kind of late to be eating.
- Where am I eating? Well, I was going to eat in the car, but now I'm going to wait until I get home.
- WHY am I eating? I'm hungry because I ate supper at 4 p.m. and I've been out all evening.
- WHY a triple cheeseburger and large fries? Because I'm craving a burger and fries.
- WHY am I having such a big serving? Because this is what I always get. Hmm, would a smaller burger and fries be enough? I suppose I could just get a regular cheeseburger, and I probably don't need the fries. Actually, if I just had some cheese and crackers when I got home, that would suffice.

I have had many clients tell me over and over again that this is a very typical dialogue that runs through their heads as they are about to turn into a drive-through. The number of times that they have changed their default choice to something completely different as they question the context of their eating has helped them make healthier choices and never feel deprived.

I hope this makes sense. The reality is there are endless ways this scenario could end simply by asking those context questions. You could realize that you are not actually hungry. You could get a smaller portion. You could decide that it is too late in the evening to have such a big meal. These questions are there to promote awareness and conscious decision-making regarding your food choices.

You can do this anywhere at any time. As you walk through the kitchen, randomly opening the fridge for no reason at all and grabbing a pop that you were not even thinking about until you saw it. Or you are cooking dinner and randomly sampling everything you are cooking. Or you are forcing yourself to eat the last three bites of a decedent cheesecake you chose at a celebratory dinner you are having with friends because you don't want to waste it.

Awareness is extremely powerful, and the cool thing about awareness is it is usually permanent. Once you exercise your awareness muscles, you will have these for life, and you will find over time, your food context eating continues to improve.

7. Abandon all negative feelings about your food decisions. Remember, Context Eating gives you full autonomy to eat whatever you DECIDE you are going to eat. EVERYTHING is ON PLAN. Rather than "eating unconsciously," you are exercising your awareness and responsibility. You no longer allow default food situations to occur without them being fully vetted. You are empowered to say "yes" or "no" to any food - joyfully and happily.

If you inevitably make a choice that doesn't feel good or that you did not feel 100% in control, learn from it. Don't beat yourself up. Ask yourself some good questions about why you felt out of control or didn't like your decision. What could you do differently next time? What parameters do you need to put in place to remain in control?

Once again, with Context Eating, there will be a learning curve. You may have a season in your life where you completely abandon all conscious food choices and go back to your default settings. But, unlike a diet, there is no all-or-nothing approach to get back to. There are only improved contexts. The point is, the more often you practice Context Eating, the more often it becomes your first nature and the more quickly you can place food back into its proper place in your life.

Now it's time to build out your Context Eating Meal Plan.

If you did the meal planning exercise back in **Chapter 8,** you already have done the following:

1. Decided on five days of regular meals.
2. Come up with five days of "occasional meals" that you will incorporate once or twice a month.
3. Come up with five days of on-the-go meals – incorporating both grab-and-go foods and foods you can get from take-out.

Now it's time to take your meal plan and add in your Context Foods.

If you know that Friday night is Pizza night, think about what you can add to that meal to add to the nutrient density and lower the impact of that meal on your blood sugar.

As mentioned previously, you could have some acacia or inulin fiber before you eat. You could add in a green salad. You could add in a shot of apple cider vinegar. You could add wings to the meal to bring up the protein content. This action task aims to put some thought into your Context Foods so that you can enjoy them without feeling guilt or deprivation.

If you add a salad and some wings to this meal, you may find you only want one piece of pizza vs. the three or four you would normally have.

Here are some additional things to think about:

If you currently have three sodas per day can you cut that down to one per day and add it to a nutrient-dense meal? After a time, that may be something that you can cut back further to "just the weekends" or "when you are out with friends".

Do the same with any of your sugary snacks or high-sugar coffees. Really think about what your non-negotiables are as you consider your health goals. Is that daily Starbucks "a must"? If so, can you alter your order in some way? Can you pair it with focus and satiating foods? Can you change "when" or "where" you are consuming this food?

Do you really enjoy that chocolate or chips at night after dinner? Great - eat it at the table vs. sitting in front of the TV.

Think about all your Context Foods and plan out how you are going to incorporate them into your meal planning. Then, stick to the plan. If you decide that you want to have your 500-calorie Starbucks drink every Friday morning, during staff meeting, paired with a low-carb Starbucks breakfast choice and a handful of almonds; then don't have it on Monday morning, in the car on the way to work, with a muffin.

Keep your commitments (promises) to yourself. Don't make a commitment you know you will never keep. If your goal is true health and weight loss, then keep that goal at the front of your mind as you begin to consciously place food back into the proper place in your life.

For this part of your meal planning write out everything that you currently eat and want to keep eating that falls under the category of Context Foods.

Then, write down the who, what, when, where, why.

Examples:

- A glass of wine with my girlfriends, Friday night, at the restaurant, because I love a glass of wine with my dinner.
- My favorite chocolate bar, with my co-workers, at the end of my lunch, at work, because I am not yet ready to give this up.

- Ice cream with my family, when we go out for ice-cream on a hot summer's day, because that is a tradition I really enjoy.
- Wendy's hamburger, with a side salad, on Monday nights, in the car, because there is no time between getting home from work and the kid's swimming class to eat.

Only you can decide what constitutes a valid context for eating your Context Foods. Again, the goal over time is to continue to "check in" with yourself on whether these are still valid contexts or are you ready to make additional changes due to a change in priorities of your health goals or even a change in your routine.

Right now you may decide that one soda a day is what you want. However, in six months time you may decide that you are ready to drop drinking soda altogether. The whole point is - you are DECIDING, vs. it being a default, unconscious, all-or-nothing action.

Take some time now to complete your meal planning before moving on to the next chapter.

CHAPTER 15

FOUNDATIONAL SUPPLEMENTS TO SUPPORT CONTEXT EATING

So far, you have learned:

1. The reasons why typical dieting and focusing only on WHAT you are eating is not sustainable and leads to yo-yo dieting and binge eating.
2. Why awareness and responsibility are the two keys empowering you to make permanent changes.
3. The four main triggers leading to disordered eating.
4. How to incorporate the first three catagories of the Context Eating Menu plan to help normalize blood sugar and leave you feeling full and satiated.
5. How to incorporate the fourth catagories of the Context Eating Menu plan and understanding why context is the most important factor in determining what you are eating.

Now I want to spend one chapter helping you understand what supplements you could start using to help you meet your health and body composition goals.

The supplements that I focus on with my clients are not "weight loss" supplements. They are supplements that support the body's physiological needs as a whole.

Remember, physiological triggers are the first triggers that need to be addressed when you are looking to stop overeating food that is causing ill health and weight gain. These are triggers caused by your body craving specific nutrients or having specific imbalances.

Adding foundational supplements to your daily regime will help ensure your body gets the nutrients it's craving. They also assist in reducing the total stress load on your body and improve underlying health markers that may influence your body's ability to release unhealthy weight.

Supplements can be used to SUPPLEMENT your diet where symptoms of deficiencies exist, and they can help to reverse a dis-ease process by providing the body "raw materials" to help it heal itself.

My basic guidelines for using supplements are as follows:

1. Supplements should not be used to counter a poor diet. This means that using supplements to replace real, nutritious focus and satiating foods is not my intention and will not lead to health transformation.

2. Supplements should never be used as a "cure-all." There is never a one size fits all.

3. Supplements should not be used without the assistance of a health practitioner. This means that you do not simply take what your friend is taking, buy what your neighbor is selling, or even use what I am suggesting unless you know they are right for you.

I had a friend recently tell me that she was stopping some supplements she had been buying from a friend representing a popular multi-level marketing company. When I asked her why she stopped the program, she said that the protein shakes gave her constant diarrhea. When I asked her how long she had been using them, she replied three months. I said, "You stayed on something for three months that gave you constant diarrhea?" and she said, "Yes, because I was told I could lose weight with these products."

This is a perfect example of what we hear from some clients who will no longer try any supplements because they have had such a bad experience with something they took that they did not receive proper guidance with.

4. Supplements should always be verified for contraindications with medications by your pharmacist, doctor, naturopathic, or functional medicine doctor.

5. With supplementation, always aim for "less is more." There will be times when you need certain protocols for specific periods of time. The more nutrients you get from your diet, and the more you manage lifestyle factors, the less you need supplements. In order to make sure that you are not taking too many supplements, it is a good idea to prioritize concerns which a qualified practitioner can help you with.

6. Supplements should not be taken "forever." There needs to be a different focus at different seasons of the year and seasons of life.

7. **Quality, form, and dosage** are three of the most important considerations when considering what supplement to take.

QUALITY:

- Is it CLEAN? – Does it have limited additives and preservatives and no common allergens or toxins? Also, consider the country of origin. There are different manufacturing standards in different counties. Canada has some of the best standards.
- Is it third-party tested to confirm that what is on the label is in the bottle in proper amounts?
- Where is it sourced?

FORM:

- Consider both the form of the supplement itself (for example, there are many forms of magnesium–oxide, citrate, bisglycinate, etc.) and what method the supplement is delivered in (for example, a capsule, soft gel, powder, liquid). Both of these need to be considered to ensure maximum assimilation (absorbency) and results.

DOSAGE:

- When looking at the dosage, consider if this dosage is right for you. You may not know, so you will need to ask. Be aware that sometimes companies will prioritize costs and marketing over therapeutic dosage. A product may say it contains a certain beneficial ingredient, but is that ingredient in a high enough dose to make a difference?

Lower-priced products will generally fall short in one of these three areas – quality, form, or dosage. However, sometimes, even more expensive products do not have the best quality, form, or dosage.

Starting with the basic supplement regime that I suggest gives people a tool that allows them to start feeling better, making some of the dietary changes they want to implement much easier.

It is easier to take a vitamin that will give you energy and help with mood than to get you to focus on removing foods you crave when you are feeling down.

When you start to feel better, you can then look at some other habits that will help with transformation and permanent change.

In the remainder of this chapter, I will discuss the basic supplements that can give you the most support, as well as important considerations for introducing and taking supplements.

I will introduce my top four choices of supplements that I suggest to everyone working through my Context Eating Program.

I choose these four basics because of their positive impact on all areas of the body and mind. These basics don't just cover up symptoms; they work to rebalance some of the underlying factors that are causing ill health and weight gain in the first place.

When used together, they can support the improvement of symptoms of energy, mood, hormonal upheaval, and more.

The four basics are:

- Omega 3 oil (fish or algae source)
- Magnesium
- Active B complex
- My Goldenroot™

These four supplements fall into four separate supplement categories.

- Healthy Fats
- Minerals
- Vitamins
- Herbs

Let's look at what each of these supplements can support in a bit more detail.

Omega 3s

Omega 3 (fish or algae source) are an essential fatty acid that you do not get enough of in your standard American diet. High-quality Omega 3s can assist with the following areas:

- Reduce inflammation – inflammation is the root cause of so many symptoms
- Brain health – both structure (cells) and mental health, including depression/anxiety/focus
- Supports healthy vision
- Supports the cardiovascular system and heart health
- Supports optimum digestion
- Improves metabolic syndrome and blood sugar balance
- Reduce symptoms of autoimmune diseases, including lupus, rheumatoid arthritis, ulcerative colitis, Crohn's disease, and psoriasis
- Supports liver health
- Supports bone and joint health
- Reduces the symptoms of PMS, including painful periods
- Improves inflammatory skin conditions

So many claims can be made about Omega 3 oils because they are building blocks to cellular health. When something is a building block to cellular health, it can improve cellular health in all parts of the body. Omega 3s improve cellular structure, and healthier cells mean healthier tissues and organs. In addition, they have strong anti-inflammatory properties that can help to reduce inflammation throughout the body. As a general rule, look for a product that is higher in EPA and take a minimum of 3000 mg per day.

Magnesium Glycinate/Bisglycinate

Magnesium is involved in over 300 different metabolic functions in the body. Because it is the catalyst (spark plug) for so many different processes, if you are deficient in magnesium, you may see a number of seemingly random symptoms.

Every cell in your body requires magnesium, and magnesium supplementation assists with:

- Brain function and mood
- Prevents insulin resistance and lowers risk for type 2 diabetes
- Reduces inflammation
- Prevents migraines
- Reduces PMS and period pain
- Improves sleep
- Lowers blood pressure
- Assists with restless leg syndrome
- Relaxes muscles
- Assists with digestion and alleviates constipation.

As you can see, supplementing with the right kind of magnesium may greatly improve many different symptoms and disease processes. The form of magnesium I most often recommend is magnesium glycinate/bisglycinate because it is bioavailable and much less likely to cause issues with diarrhea.

Look for a product that specifically says glycinate or bisglycinate on the package.

Active B Complex

The third supplement that is part of my basic recommendations is an Active B complex. "Active" means that the b vitamins are already in a form that is ready to be used by the body. There is no conversion or activation necessary. This is important because many people may be missing some of the cofactors that are necessary to activate some B vitamins. So if you are one of these people and are taking an inactive form, the vitamin may remain inert and not be doing you any good.

B vitamins assist with

- Improving the health of cells, specifically red blood cells, which equals more oxygen and nutrients in circulation
- Increased energy
- Improved sleep and dream recall
- Improved digestion
- Support nerve function
- Support an improved response to stress
- Support mood
- Support the health of the skin
- Support the immune system
- Support focus and concentration

I love B vitamins because, unlike many other supplements, you can often see immediate benefits from taking B vitamins, like improved energy and focus the very first day you take them. B vitamins are water-soluble, and your requirement for them increases significantly when you are under stress or on certain medications. B vitamins act as a "stress buffer, " which is why they remain in my top 4. Look for a product that specifically says "Active" B complex. Some brands that clients have used include AOR, Genestra, Natural Factors, and Lorna Vanderhaeghe.

My Goldenroot™

The final supplement in my basic 4 is my favorite because I personally formulated this product and have clients across the globe who are now using it. It contains healing organic herbs and spices and is fermented, offering incredible digestive system benefits. Organic fermented turmeric, ginger, oregano, black pepper, and lavender work together to help reduce inflammation, improve digestion, support the immune system, helps heal leaky gut and support so many different systems of the body. My Goldenroot™ is only available through me directly at https://bit.ly/3Hp9GzU

It is done in small batches and is not mass-produced. Made in a Canadian approved lab.

- The fermentation process makes it very bioavailable
- The ingredients are known anti-inflammatories
- It supports healthy digestion

- Improved gut health leads to better immune function
- Improved liver health helps with detoxification processes
- Anti-inflammatory properties positively impact brain health

These are my top four basic supplements that I most commonly suggest when people are trying to lose weight and increase their health because they all support all areas of the body and address many of the root causes that lead to weight gain. They are also safe and effective for most people to use with most medications. (Please refer to the upcoming section on cautions and contraindications for more information.)

How to introduce your supplements

Most people do not know how to introduce new supplements into their routine correctly and when supplements are incorrectly introduced, you can end up with some problems, including avoidable side effects. Be sure to follow these suggestions to avoid unwanted issues.

Supplements should be introduced one at a time with a space of a minimum of three days separating any new supplement. The reason you do this is twofold. 1. If there is any reaction, it is easier to identify which supplement is causing the problem. 2. You will have a better idea of what the individual supplement is doing for you (eg., if you start feeling really energetic after you start taking the Active B complex, you will know it is the Bs).

Side effects are extremely rare with these supplements, but if you experience any nausea, heartburn, diarrhea, or anything else that you are concerned about, discontinue use and connect with your healthcare provider.

The majority of supplements should be taken with food. Taking your supplements with food is important for a couple of reasons. First, it can reduce any potential nausea, heartburn, or repeating of the supplement. Second, the body will be more likely to assimilate the supplement if it is taken with food because vitamins, minerals, fats, etc., are a part of food. There is nothing in nature where the body would receive isolated B vitamins or magnesium apart from food, so taking it with food is a natural way for a supplement to be digested.

Supplements should not be taken near any medications, either over the counter or prescription, and certain supplements should not be taken near each other. Always take your supplements a minimum of two hours away from any of your medications.

To make it easier not to forget to take your supplements, take them at the same time each day. Most people find that they usually remember to take their supplements at breakfast but often forget to take any that are scheduled for later in the day. So as much as possible, take them at breakfast.

The basics that I have suggested to you can all be taken together at the same time as they do not interact with each other.

As B vitamins can be energizing, I suggest that you take your active B before 4 p.m. to avoid any interaction with sleep.

Although these four basic supplements are generally safe to take with many medications, it is your responsibility to confirm with your pharmacist or doctor. More problematic medications include any kind of blood thinner, anti-seizure medications, or any other medications where you have had issues regulating the proper dose. Other special considerations include allergy to certain ingredients such as fish or lavender.

Please remember that all supplements I suggest are just that, suggestions. I give you all the information as a nutritionist who has received untold hours of training on supplementation and worked with thousands of people over the last 20+ years, but it is up to you to confirm these products are right for you.

To recap, it is important that you introduce and take your supplements as directed to help ensure the best results. The basic supplements that I am suggesting for you, to begin with, will be a good choice for most people.

CONCLUSION

WRAPPING IT ALL UP

Now in terms of what you can expect in terms of weight loss rate and how long that weight stays off, that is all dependent upon you and how dedicated you are to improving your eating contexts.

When they start reincorporating their favorite Context Foods, some people initially go back to eating them in excess. If this happens to you, don't panic. This is the time to dig in and evaluate the WHYs and then come up with solutions. Take a very close look at your triggers, especially the physiological ones, and determine what changes you need.

You can't permanently solve a problem if you don't take the time to figure out what is causing the problem. You need to become a detective and get a little obsessive about self-reflection. Just don't get stuck in self-reflection and forget to take action.

Remember, it's not enough to say, "Okay, from now on, I will only eat the chocolate cake within the context of a celebration like a birthday party." You must also back that up with actions. Maybe actions such as "no cake or anything that looks like cake comes into the house." The difference between this and simply telling yourself you will never eat cake again is that you can absolutely look forward to eating cake at your next birthday party.

If it's donuts at work that are your struggle, and you can't actually distance yourself from them because people keep bringing them in, go through your mental checklist. Who, what, when, where, why. Ask yourself how much you REALLY want that donut, or is it simply because it is there? Ask yourself what you would prefer to have if you had to choose: a glass of wine with dinner or a donut. Decide which is more important to you and say no to the "good" option to enjoy the "best" option.

Context Eating is about balancing your goals with your desire to enjoy certain foods. As your goals and life circumstances change, your Context Eating parameters can also change. There may be seasons in your life where you need or want to have more strict parameters and other seasons in your life where you need or want to have less strict parameters. YOU are in control. YOU decide.

One thing to remember is you always want to add in something before you take something away, and you want to get to the root of the symptom. Overeating unhealthy foods is just a symptom. There is always a root issue at play. It is nearly impossible to control your food cravings if your blood sugar levels are dysregulated, or you are missing nutrients in your diet. Eating more focus foods, satiating foods, and nutrient-dense carbohydrates in addition to your foundational supplements will keep you satiated so that you don't have the same uncontrollable cravings.

If you are craving something, eat it right after a meal containing the first 2 or 3 catagories while sitting at a table. I know I have said it before, but the goal is to break the situational pattern and other associations that accompany the food craving. Don't say no to the food that you really really want. Start by changing the context you are eating it in. For instance, if you usually have a high-carb or high-sugar snack in the middle of the day, move that specific food to the end of a meal.

Keep your emotions out of all your decisions, questions, analysis, and even your "failures." You must approach this like you are dedicating yourself to solving a problem, and you will collect information, analyze it, experiment, evaluate the conclusion, and move on. This will not work if you continue to call yourself names, become dramatic about the gain of a pound or two, or react with complete despair if you once again stare at the bottom of an extra large 1000-calorie creamy chocolate chill.

If that happens, say, "Well, that was interesting – let's find out what went wrong there. Too often, we expect to be good at something right away and that we should have success right away. The world rarely works that way. Don't give up. Be willing to take the long road to permanent success with its inevitable detours along the way.

This leads to the next reminder. Continue your mind growth. Remember that your mind is the boss of your body. If your body truly believes what your mind tells it, it will act and behave according to the belief, for better or worse. If you have identified yourself as sick, unhealthy, or fat, your body will respond accordingly. If you affirm to your body that you are getting healthier and healthier every day, this can be very powerful for moving your health in the right direction.

Also, remember that we are working on root and environment-level issues. This means you may not initially see the incredible outward transformation you desire. Building a foundation of a healthy environment and roots takes time. You need to trust the process and continue to work on your root level issues while you apply the foundations of the Context Eating Method.

In conclusion, I want to talk for a moment about my personal Context Eating because I think it will be helpful for some.

What I want you to understand about me is that I have a serious sweet tooth. If left to my whims, I would eat cookies, cake, ice cream, and chocolate every day, all day long. It's not even funny. I would also weigh a lot more than I do and be very unhealthy if I had not learned how to apply Context Eating many years ago.

I have done all the "I will never eat sugar again" programs and detoxes. They work for a couple of days, weeks, and one time even a few months, but eventually, I get back onto sugar, and when I do, I go overboard. Plus, I have no other vices. I don't drink, smoke, or do drugs. Eating my mom's chocolate chip cookies or a decadent homemade brownie brings me joy, and I am not ready to give that up.

I have had to set up some pretty strict Context Eating parameters. When I go grocery shopping once per week, I buy myself one very expensive 100-gram chocolate bar. This chocolate bar might last me one day or a few days. It doesn't matter; I only get one. Pieces of this chocolate bar are eaten directly after my meals while sitting at the table. I've learned that I can't have ice cream or anything else sweet in the house, not even a bag of semi-sweet chocolate chips, or I won't stay away from them.

Apart from that one chocolate bar, all my other sweets are eaten outside my home with friends or family, at restaurants, or at social events. The only other time that there are sweets in my home is around Christmas.

Is this 100% true? No, not 100%, though I am getting close. There are life events that can cause setbacks. Take the pandemic, for instance. The restaurants were closed for months, and I wasn't seeing family or friends, so I was bored. I started bringing sweets home again, and in the first six months of the lockdowns, I gained back some unwanted weight.

But, even while I was doing that, I was asking questions. Why did I decide to buy that pint of ice cream? Why did I just grab that snack at 11 p.m. and eat it in my bed? By answering these questions ("Oh, you were hungry when you were grocery shopping," or "Oh, you missed getting enough focus foods in" or "Oh, you haven't been taking your omega 3 supplement," or "Oh, life really feels sucky right now"), the poor Context Eating events went down again. Within a short time, I moved back into balance.

Will this method help me reach the point where my body fat percentage is in my optimum range and I am back into size four clothes? Maybe not, but that is not my goal right now. If that were my goal, I would be stricter with my portions and Context Foods. But my goal right now is to be healthier at 50 than I was at 40, and I am well on my way without sucking all the glutinous and chocolate-filled joy from my life.

Those of us who think about food all day long and have addictive tendencies need a different approach to managing our food intake to keep ourselves at a weight where we feel comfortable and happy. We need to drop judgment from those who say, "Just put down your fork."

We need to embrace our beautiful bodies without allowing ourselves to continue down a path completely at odds with our health. The more information you consciously collect about your habits and triggers, the more you will continue to move in the right direction. My hope for you, and the whole reason I wrote this book, is that you eliminate the all-or-nothing approaches that never work and silence the destructive voices that lead to a disordered relationship with food.

Through Context Eating, we can begin to change the dieting narrative. What will get you further ahead: losing 100 pounds and regaining 140, or losing 50 pounds and keeping it off for good?

- Let's normalize your "goal weight" being above your "ideal weight."
- Let's celebrate losing 50 pounds and keeping it off, even when society says you should lose 100 pounds.
- Let's stop demonizing the foods you love to eat and put them back into contexts that lead you to greater health and well-being.
- Let's work at your health goals over decades, not weeks.
- Let's normalize setbacks and learning curves without feeling like a complete failure.
- Let's recognize that different stages of life result in different body sizes and health priorities.
- Let's change how the world does weight loss.

And from now on, if anyone asks you if you are on a diet, you can say, "No, I don't diet, I Context Eat".

AUTHORS NOTE

Thank you for reading The Context Eating Method for Women

It is our deep desire to support the middle majority of women looking for a replacement for dieting and the "all or nothing" approaches they inevitably fall into.

We believe Context Eating offers a third approach that acknowledges the disservice that the "all or nothing" choices do to most women. Context Eating offers learnable eating parameters that give women guidance to make healthier choices so that they can lose weight over time or even stop their weight from continuing to climb to unhealthier levels as they get older.

We hope that you find the fresh perspective Context Eating offers to be a gift on your journey to better health, well-being, and wholeness!

If you have found this new approach to be helpful or insightful, would you be willing to post an honest review of The Context

Eating Method - How to Lose Weight without Sucking the Gluten, Chocolate, and Wine-Filled Joy from your Life?

Our big goal is to "Change how the world does weight loss," and when you post a review, it helps other women just like you find our book and begin applying the Context Eating strategies to their lives.

To do so, simply go to the website where you purchased the book and submit a review.

We thank you so much!

We wish you health and wholeness in all areas of your life!

Darpan and Kathy

BONUS CONTENT

Awareness is the first step in the foundation for permanent change. If you want to make lasting changes, you need to get to the root of the issue vs. simply trying to patch the problem.

Awareness helps you understand why you overeat. To understand the WHY behind your overeating, you need to understand your overeating triggers.

What you will receive:

The Triggered Eating Inventory is a tool we give to anyone who wants to learn how to apply Context Eating to their life.

It helps to identify the most significant liabilities regarding food-related triggers. These triggers are grouped into four basic categories.

1. Physiological
2. Emotional
3. Situational
4. Habitual

Once you have completed the quiz, you can read through the accompanying information and strategies in each section to learn how to manage and/or avoid these triggers.

You will also gain insight into why diets that only try to change your habits don't work.

You can repeat this quiz every few months to better understand your changes and progress as you learn how to ditch dieting and incorporate Context Eating into your life.

Go here now to receive this valuable bonus included with the book. Enjoy! www.luckybookpublishing.com/contexteating

MEAL PLAN EXAMPLES AND RECIPES

Here is a list of meal examples to get you eating the same way we teach in our Context Eating Program. This list will get you thinking about how to incorporate Focus, Satiating and Comfort Foods at each meal. Remember, the whole goal of Context Eating Meal Planning is to get away from adherence to a strict diet plan and learn how to pair foods to:

1. Meet the physiological/nutritional needs of the body to reduce cravings
2. Regulate dysregulated blood sugars by increasing focus and satiating foods.

Some of these examples are more nutrient-dense and balanced than others. The goal is never perfection. The goal is to make sustainable changes to the who,what,when, where, why of your food contexts.

You will notice that some of the breakfast ideas are not typical breakfast foods. This is to get you thinking outside of the typical high-carb, over-processed cereal box standard North American choices. These are just ideas. You need to take the examples and make them your own. "Mix and match" and always be thinking about ways you can add even more Focus Foods to your meals.

When you want to enjoy your Context Foods, begin with these nutrient-dense, satiating ideas and then incorporate your context foods.

We have also included a section called "Darpan's favorite recipes". These are nutrient-dense meals that are family favorites in our homes and we share regularly with our clients.

Breakfast Ideas

1. Bone broth – add bok choy; cilantro; mushrooms; pair with cooked broccoli with butter;1 egg; avocado; sea salt
2. Hot water with lemon and ginger; 1 boiled egg; pair with ½ cup of oatmeal with 1 tablespoon of almond butter mixed in
3. Sweet potato toast (recipe) with 1 or 2 eggs, avocado, cooked asparagus
4. Green tea with lemon, 2 eggs, bacon, sauerkraut
5. Chicken breast cooked in ghee or butter; add your favorite herbs, arugula, cucumbers, onion
6. 2 egg omelet with spinach; mushroom; cheese ½ bagel with butter

7. Chia pudding (recipe) paired with toast and peanut butter

8. Sauerkraut mixed with chopped bacon and apple, sea salt, pepper

9. Raspberry Banana Smoothie (recipe)

10. 1 boiled egg, 1 slice of cheddar cheese, cucumber slices paired with inulin or acacia fiber and moringa leaf powder in water

11. Starbucks low-carb breakfast choices, green tea, apple cider vinegar shot

12. "Bullet-proof" coffee paired with Banana Bread (recipe) and choice of protein

13. ½ toasted english muffin with smoked salmon and avocado

14. ½ toasted english muffin with nut butter, celery sticks; pair with inulin or acacia fiber

15. Bone broth with added chicken, cilantro, herbs, spices

16. ½ cup oatmeal add cinnamon, pumpkin seeds, cashews; pair with protein

17. McDonald's or AandW breakfast sandwich; pair with moringa and inulin or acacia fiber

18. 1 tin of sardines or mackerel; pair with store-bought kale salad

19. Choice of protein shake paired with veggies and dip

20. 1 slice french toast with bacon or sausage, 1 or 2 eggs, apple cider vinegar shot

Lunch Ideas

1. 1 tin of tuna with mayo, celery, onion, pair with Squash Soup (recipe)
2. Caesar salad with romaine, bacon, parmesan, dressing and chicken
3. Sliced lunch meat with quinoa salad (various online recipes)
4. Full-fat greek yogurt with ¼ cup of blueberries
5. Pizza wrap – Tortilla wrap with sauce; meat; vegetables; cheese paired with your favorite green salad and dressing
6. Anti-inflammatory carrot lentil soup (recipe) paired with additional protein
7. Tuna melt - ½ can tuna with mayo on 2 halves of english muffin add cheese and tomato and toast in the oven
8. Chicken wings; green salad; dressing; sour cream; sweet potato fries
9. Hamburger patty with green salad and dressing
10. ½ Sandwich paired with large portion of raw veggies and dip; add a deviled egg for additional protein
11. 1 or 2 beef or chicken fajitas with cheese, avocado, salsa and lettuce
12. Shrimp or scallops paired with a green salad
13. Smoked salmon on a ½ bagel with cream cheese; pair with veggies and dip
14. Leftovers from the previous night's supper

15. Chicken or beef shawarma plate with salad– limit the rice and potato (these portions are often big enough to eat over two meals)
16. Cold cuts, boiled egg, raw veggies and hummus
17. Chicken breast paired with creamy cauliflower (recipe)
18. Your choice of protein paired with chia pudding (recipe)
19. No-bake protein bars (recipe) paired with green salad
20. Cashew cream dip (recipe) paired with raw veggies

Supper Ideas

1. Turkey stuffed peppers (recipe)
2. Chicken thighs paired with cauliflower rice (recipe) and steamed asparagus
3. Garbonzo veggie stir-fry (recipe)
4. Gluten-free crusted fish (recipe) paired with broccoli or asparagus
5. Greek souvlaki with Greek salad, olives, dressing (restaurant)
6. Back ribs with ½ cup mashed potatoes, Brussels sprouts or cauliflower
7. Shirataki/ Konjak noodles with meat sauce paired with caesar salad
8. Striploin steak with fried mushrooms, bok choy, onions and cashews paired with a green salad
9. Beef or lamb stew paired with asparagus or other focus food
10. Garlic Spaghetti squash (recipe) paired with meat sauce and salad

11. Lamb Rogan (recipe) paired with ¼ cup rice or ½ naan bread
12. Bacon and eggs paired with homefries and sauerkraut
13. Stuffed chicken breast (cheese, broccoli) with raw veggies and dip
14. Salmon filet; roasted vegetable medley – Beets; peppers; tomato; sweet potato; onion; zucchini; olive oil and lemon
15. Roast beef; Gravy from drippings; small potato; green salad; olive oil; apple cider vinegar and herbs
16. Pulled pork and broccoli salad (bacon, mayonnaise, sunflower seeds; green onion)
17. Taco salad – Romaine; ground beef; spices; peppers; cheese; sour cream; avocado; salsa; tomato and corn chips
18. "Shepherd's pie" made with mashed cauliflower instead of potato, paired with salad or raw vegetables
19. Chicken stir-fry cashew, with peppers, onions, bok choy, mushrooms, and other veggies. Pair with ½ cup rice
20. Salmon filet paired with asparagus drizzled in butter and sea salt

Snack Ideas

1. Apple with almond butter
2. Cottage cheese with cucumbers or peppers
3. Veggies and dip
4. Chocolate avocado pudding (recipe)
5. Fat bombs (recipes online)

6. Trail mix
7. Protein shake
8. Chia pudding
9. Apple with cinnamon paired with cheese
10. Plain greek yogurt with blueberries
11. Bone broth with added meat or vegetables
12. Cold meat paired with cucumber or peppers
13. Toast with (natural) peanut butter
14. Marys crackers, cheese string, kohlrabi
15. Celery, kohlrabi with hummus
16. Inulin or acacia fiber with moringa and raspberries in the blender
17. Mary's crackers with almond butter
18. Plain greek yogurt with chia and flax seeds
19. No-bake protein bars (recipe)
20. Tea with lemon (because sometimes you aren't actually hungry)

DARPAN'S FAVORITE RECIPES

SWEET POTATO TOAST

Sweet potato toast is a delicious way to switch up your breakfast routine. Just slice a sweet potato, bake it in the oven, and top it with fresh ingredients. It's as easy as that!

Preheat your oven to 400 degrees Fahrenheit

Slice the potato lengthwise into even slices (approximately 1/4 to 1/2-inch thick). Then place them onto a parchment-lined baking sheet. Bake for 30 minutes or until slightly toasted.

Thicker slices require more time.

Place your toppings on, and you're done!

*Note: you can lightly oil the sweet potato toast before baking, if you'd like.

Tips:

Choose orange and red-skinned potatoes. These are known as the "moist varieties" and tend to be sweeter, creamier, and less starchy.

Don't be confused with yams. Sometimes the red and orange-skinned potatoes can be labeled as yams. While yams can certainly be used, they're a bit starchy and dry. Great source of Potassium; Vitamin A; Fibre; Iron; Calcium; Selenium; Vitamin B; Vitamin C

CHIA PUDDING

It is so easy to make chia pudding! And remember net carbs? Well, 2 tablespoons of chia seeds have 12 grams of carbs but 11 grams of fiber, so only 1 gram of net carbs!

Ingredients

- 1/2 cup coconut milk
- 2 tablespoons chia
- 1/4 teaspoon of vanilla

Directions

Mix the ingredients in a mason jar or any glass container (a whisk works best). Store in the refrigerator overnight. Eat the next morning plain or top with berries for extra fiber and nutrients, or top with hemp seeds for added protein *if you don't like coconut milk, any unsweetened milk can be used.

Aside from the protein, fiber, antioxidants, and omega-3s, some studies suggest that chia seeds have additional health benefits, including weight loss, reduced inflammation, and reduced blood sugar, and may even lower the risk of heart disease.

RASPBERRY BANANA SMOOTHIE

Ingredients

- 2 tsp ground flax seeds
- 1/2 cup almond or oat milk
- 1/2 cup of water
- 1/3 of a ripe banana
- 1/2 cup frozen raspberries
- 1 scoop of protein powder
- 1 tablespoon almond butter (optional)
- 3 ice cubes

Directions

Combine all ingredients in a blender. Mix for one minute and serve immediately.

NO BAKE PROTEIN BARS

Ingredients

- 1 cup of raw creamy almond butter
- 3 tablespoons melted coconut oil
- 1/2 teaspoon vanilla extract
- 1 scoop of protein
- 1/2 tablespoon cinnamon
- 1 tablespoon flax seeds
- 1 tablespoon chia seeds
- 2 tablespoons unsweetened coconut flakes
- 1/2 cup chopped almonds

Instructions

In a large bowl, whisk together the almond butter, coconut oil and vanilla. Add in the protein, cinnamon, flax seeds, chia seeds, unsweetened coconut flakes, and chopped almonds. Use a rubber spatula to fold in all of the ingredients. Line a loaf pan with parchment paper and pour the batter in. Freeze for 2 hours, then cut into bars. Store in the freezer until you are ready to eat them

ANTI-INFLAMMATORY CARROT LENTIL SOUP

Ingredients

- 1 tablespoon coconut oil (or olive oil)
- 1 large onion, minced

- 3 carrots, peeled and chopped into 1" chunks
- 1 sweet potato, peeled and chopped into 1" chunks
- 2 teaspoons of allspice
- 1/2 teaspoon cayenne pepper
- 1 cup red lentils
- 6 cups vegetable broth
- juice from 1/2 lemon

Optional Toppings

- chives
- parsley
- pumpkin seeds

Directions

In a large pot, heat the coconut oil over medium-high. Add the onions, carrots, and sweet potato. Cook, constantly stirring, for 10 minutes, or until just beginning to brown, then add all the spice and cayenne and cook for 2 more minutes or until the spices are fragrant. Add lentils and broth and bring to a boil. Reduce heat to low and simmer, covered, for 40 minutes or until sweet potatoes are tender and lentils are cooked. Pulse in a food processor or blender until ingredients are combined, but soup still has texture.

GARBANZO-VEGGIE STIR-FRY

This satisfying vegetarian dinner incorporates vegetables, garbanzo beans, heart-healthy olive oil, and fresh herbs.

Ingredients

- 1 15-ounce can of garbanzo beans, drained and rinsed
- 1 large zucchini, halved and sliced
- ½ cup of fresh mushrooms, sliced
- 1 ripe tomato, chopped
- 1 clove of garlic, crushed
- 1 tablespoon of fresh cilantro, chopped
- 1 tablespoon of fresh basil, chopped
- 1 tablespoon of fresh oregano, chopped
- Freshly ground black pepper to taste
- 2 tablespoons of olive oil

Directions

Heat the olive oil in a large skillet over medium-low heat. Stir in the garlic, basil, oregano, and pepper. Add the zucchini and garbanzo beans. Stir well to coat with oil and herbs. Cover and cook for 19 minutes, stirring occasionally. Stir in mushrooms and cilantro. Cook until tender, stirring occasionally. Put the chopped tomato over the top of the mixture, cover, and let it steam for a few minutes. Serve immediately.

TURKEY STUFFED PEPPERS

Ingredients

- Bell peppers
- Turkey
- Yellow onion, chopped

- Minced garlic
- Cooked quinoa or brown rice
- Black pepper
- Gluten-free creole seasoning
- Shredded parmesan cheese
- Fresh thyme or rosemary for garnish

Directions

Preheat your oven to 400 F. Cut off the top of 4 bell peppers (clean out the inside and de-seed) and dice up the 5th pepper. Set aside the diced pepper. In a square baking dish, add ½ inch of water to the bottom and then add the 4 bell peppers. Place this in the oven to bake (this helps turn the peppers into a tender, crispy pepper versus and crispy-crispy pepper!) while you are preparing the turkey/quinoa mix. Heat the turkey in a large skillet until cooked thoroughly (may need a TBSP of oil for this step). Add the onions and diced bell pepper just before the turkey is fully cooked and allow to cook until the veggies start to soften approximately 2-3 minutes. Add in the minced garlic and cook for 1 minute. Mix in the rice well and then add in creole seasoning. Remove from heat. Place the rice mixture evenly into the four bell peppers. Top each pepper with 1 TBSP of cheese and garnish with a bit of thyme. Bake for 25-30 minutes or until the cheesy tops turn golden brown. Enjoy!

CAULIFLOWER RICE – (PAIR WITH YOUR CHOICE OF PROTEIN)

Ingredients

- 1 large head of cauliflower
- Sea salt and pepper to taste
- 1/4 cup of coconut oil
- Cilantro 1/4 – 1/3 cup finely chopped

Directions

Shred head of cauliflower in food processor. Melt coconut oil in a large frying pan on medium low heat; add shredded cauliflower and salt and pepper. Keep turning cauliflower with oil until thoroughly heated. Before serving, mix in cilantro. Try other ingredients such as sautéed oils and finely diced vegetables. A fantastic rice replacement!

SQUASH SOUP (PAIR WITH FOCUS FOOD, PROTEIN, AND FAT)

Ingredients

- 1 large butternut squash roasted (skin removed)
- 1 tbsp. butter or ghee
- 1 large onion peeled and chopped
- White pepper and Sea Salt to taste
- 4 -6 cups water with 1 vegetable broth cube
- 1 clove garlic roasted

- 2 tsp. grated fresh ginger

Directions

Roast garlic with squash, cut side down in the oven on a cookie sheet with ½ cup water at 350F until soft. In a large pot; sauté onion in butter or ghee until transparent add ginger, water, and broth cube. When the squash is cooked, remove the seeds and then scoop out the cooked squash and add to the pot. Squeeze garlic cloves into a pot. Puree using a plunge blender or in a blender, then return to the pot to heat. The squash seeds can also be dry-roasted with a little sea salt.

GLUTEN FREE BREADED CRUSTED FISH

Ingredients

- 1/2 cup salted almonds
- 1/4 cup gluten-free breadcrumbs, plain or seasoned
- 2-4 fish thin filets (salmon, cod, other)
- 1/4 cup Dijon mustard
- 1–2 tablespoons grapeseed oil
- 1 tablespoon butter
- parmesan cheese, fresh lemon, or Himalayan for topping

Directions

Place the almonds and breadcrumbs in a food processor and pulse until coarsely ground into a crumb-like mixture. Place the crumb mixture on a plate or in a shallow bowl. Heat oil and butter in a frying pan over medium-high heat. Spread each filet with 1 tablespoon Dijon mustard on both sides. Press the fish into the crumbs to get it coated on both sides. I do this several times to ensure the whole thing gets covered. Place the fish into the frying pan and cook for several minutes on each side until the outside is browned and the fish is fully cooked. I usually just check the middle of the fish for doneness – pieces will flake off easily when it's done.

Serve with parmesan, sea salt or lemon.

GARLIC SPAGHETTI SQUASH - PAIR WITH YOUR FAVORITE MEAT SAUCE

Ingredients

- 1 small spaghetti squash about 3-4 pounds
- 2 tablespoons butter
- 2 cloves garlic finely minced
- 1/4 cup finely minced parsley or other fresh herb
- 1/2 teaspoon salt or to taste 1/4 cup shredded parmesan cheese

Directions

Preheat the oven to 375 F. Pierce squash a few times with a sharp paring knife (to let steam escape). Bake spaghetti squash for 60 minutes or until a paring knife pierces easily through skin with little resistance. Let squash cool for 10 minutes. Cut squash in half, lengthwise. Use a fork to remove and discard the seeds. Continue using a fork to scrape the squash to get long, lovely strands. If the squash seems difficult to scrape, place squash halves cut side down, and bake for an additional 10 minutes. To serve 4 people, you'll use about 4 cups of the spaghetti squash strands. Heat a large saute pan with the butter and the garlic over medium low heat. When garlic becomes fragrant, add parsley, salt and spaghetti squash strands. Toss well, sprinkle in the parmesan cheese and taste to see if you need additional salt. The spaghetti squash should have a slight crunch - but if you like it softer, cover the pan and cook for 2 more minutes. Voila!

CREAMY CAULIFLOWER

Ingredients

- Sauce 2 3/4 cups water
- 1/2 cup raw soaked cashews
- 1 156ml can tomato paste
- 1 tbsp garam masala
- 1 tsp chilli powder
- 1 tsp ground cumin
- 1 tsp himalayan salt
- 1 tsp lemon juice
- 1/2 tsp powdered ginger

Directions

Blend all together in a blender Cauliflower Main 2 tbsp coconut oil 1 medium yellow onion chopped 5 cloves pureed garlic 1 medium cauliflower head, cut into florets Saute main ingredients then add sauce. Simmer for 30 mins. Serve with protein.

LAMB ROGAN

Ingredients

- 400 g Lamb Shoulder
- 1 tbsp Ghee butter, lamb fat or olive oil
- 1 Star Anise
- 1/2 tsp Cumin Seeds
- 1/2 tsp Fennel Seeds
- 5 Cardamom Pods
- 1 lrg Onion
- 1/2 tsp Cinnamon
- 1 tsp Coriander Powder
- 1/2 tsp Chilli Powder
- 1/2 tsp Paprika
- 1/2 tsp Cayenne Pepper

Directions

Chop your lamb shoulder into bite-size pieces and season with salt. Mix together your star anise, 1/2 tsp cumin seeds, 1/2 tsp fennel seeds, and 5 cardamom pods, then set aside in a small container. Powder, 1/2 tsp paprika and 1/2 tsp cayenne pepper and set aside in another small container. In a blender or pestle and mortar, blend or smash together your fresh ginger and garlic. Set aside in a small bowl. In a very hot pan with some of your ghee, sear the edges of the meat all over and set aside.

1. Dice an onion as finely as you can and fry in ghee or animal fat on a low-medium temperature for 6 – 8 minutes, seasoning with salt.

2. After 8 minutes, make a little space in the pan for your whole spices and add them in. Allow them to make direct contact with the hot pan for 30 seconds or so, before mixing them in with the onions for a further minute and a half.

3. Do the same as above, but this time with the spice mix you made earlier. First adding it to a relatively clear part of the pan for 30 seconds or so and then mix it in with the onions and allow another minute and a half.

4. Now add the paste you made earlier. Mix it in with the onions and allow it to cook for a couple of minutes.

5. Move everything from the pan to a blender and combine thoroughly, then switch back to the pan.

6. Add the meat back in and stir together. Optionally, add fresh chillies as well.

7. Add the stock and a bay leaf and allow it to reduce slowly over the course of an hour or two. Once the sauce is at the desired consistency and the meat is sufficiently tender,

8. Mix together your 1/2 tsp cinnamon, 1 tsp coriander powder, and 1/2 tsp chilli you're ready to serve!

9. Plate up and garnish with coriander and lime juice. Or with nothing at all!

10. Serve with ¼ cup rice or ½ naan bread.

CASHEW CREAM DIP

Ingredients

- 1 cup raw cashews, soaked at least 2 hours if not overnight
- ¼ cup filtered water
- ¼ cup raw coconut nectar (or maple syrup, yacon, agave nectar)
- Pinch Himalayan crystal salt
- 1 heaped teaspoon raw coconut oil
- 1 teaspoon vanilla extract (or ground organic vanilla beans)
- Few squirts of fresh squeezed lemon juice from 1 lemon

Directions

Blend the mixture all together in a food processor until it is as smooth as possible. Serve with crackers or vegetables. Store in a closed container in the fridge.

KOHLRABI

Kohlrabi This unusual but tasty vegetable has the delicious flavors of cabbage, radish and broccoli. It's available year-round from your local grocery store, a great side to any meal or snack option. Give it a try…your body will thank you

- a low-calorie, high-fiber focus food
- lots of minerals and vitamins, especially potassium and vitamin C
- prostate and colon cancer protective (cruciferous family)
- keeps well in the fridge for a few days even when cut up

Kohlrabi can be used raw; just cut off the top and bottom, then the green outer skin. Can be sliced into thick pieces or grated into a salad. Most kids enjoy the crunch and mild flavor. Keep some cut up for a quick healthy snack for the whole family. Great with a dip too. Kohlrabi can also be cooked; simply peel and cut into cubes. Place in ½" of boiling water, cover, and simmer until soft (approx. 7 minutes). Drain and toss with butter or olive oil, salt, and pepper. It's also delicious in soup

PROTEIN BITES ON THE GO

Ingredients

- 2/3 cup any butter (I like the Batches stone ground peanut, macadamia, cashew mix blend butter)
- 1/2 cup semi-sweet chocolate chips (other variations are Dark Chocolate Chips Shredded Coconut Cranberries)
- 1 cup old-fashioned oats (if you are gluten-free Bob's red makes it)
- 1/2 cup ground flax seeds (other variations are Chopped Walnuts, Pecans or Almonds, Hemp Seeds, and chia Seeds)

- 1 tablespoon honey I like True bee (other variations maple syrup, agave nectar, rice syrup, coconut sugar (sugar alternatives stevia, erythritol)

Directions

Combine all 5 ingredients in a medium bowl. Stir to combine. Place in the refrigerator for 15-30 minutes so they are easier to roll. Roll into 12 bites and store in the fridge for up to a week. Voila!

AVOCADO CHOCOLATE PUDDING

Ingredients:

- One large avocado
- 1/4 cup cocoa powder
- 1/4 cup nut milk
- 1/4 cup honey I put less (I use TrueBee by Peachey Honey Farm)
- One teaspoon of vanilla

Directions:

Using the amounts above, you end up with a dark chocolate-style mousse. Not too sweet! If you'd like a more milk chocolate flavor, I suggest using a little less cocoa powder and more honey.

Put everything into a food processor or blender. Break the avocado up into smaller pieces to make it easier on your machine.

Process for 10-15 seconds and then stop and scrape down the sides. Then process again until nice and smooth.

You can eat it right away or chill for a little while before you dig in.

I just wouldn't let it sit too long in the fridge - once the avocado starts oxidizing like crazy it will alter the flavor, and not in a good way…

VEGAN BANANA BREAD

No sugar added and gluten-free.

Dry Ingredients

- 2 cups of Oat Flour
- 2 teaspoons Golden root powder blend(optional)
- 2 teaspoons of baking powder aluminum free
- 1 teaspoon Ceylon cinnamon
- 1 teaspoon nutmeg
- ½ teaspoon celtic salt

Wet Ingredients

- ¾ cup non-dairy milk (i use coconut)
- ¾ cup of coconut oil
- 10 large Medjool dates (pitted) cr figs
- 3 ripe bananas
- 1 tablespoon apple cider vinegar

- 1 teaspoon real vanilla extract
- ½ cup chopped walnuts (optional)

Directions

Preheat the oven to 350 F. Lightly grease an 8" X 4" loaf pan then line with parchment paper. In a large bowl whisk together all the dry ingredients.

In a blender, blend together the non-dairy milk, bananas, dates, apple cider vinegar, and vanilla extract until all the dates are pureed.

Add the blended mixture to the dry ingredients and whisk together. Then add the coconut oil and mix it together.

Pour batter into the loaf pan. Sprinkle the chopped walnuts along the top. Bake for 120 mins until golden brown. Test by inserting a toothpick in the center. If the toothpick comes out clean, then the banana bread is ready.

TIPS FOR MAKING A GREAT BONE BROTH STOCK

Find beef bones that come from grass-fed cows and are fairly large with big thick tubes of marrow (1 lb. worth). Try not to get too tall ones, making it hard to get all that healthy marrow out!

Make sure to sprinkle both sides of the bones with salt and pepper, place them in a baking pan with a bit of a rim- this will catch those drops of liquid gold also known as fat.

Roast the bones at 400 F for 10-15 minutes, not too long or you will completely melt the marrow down and we don't want that.

Place bones and water (just cover the bones) in a pot then add 2 tbsp of apple cider vinegar. This helps pull out the important nutrients from the bones. Fill a stock pot with 8 cups of water, and slowly bring to a boil with bones added to boiling water. Here's the easy part, I just dump everything in... Salt, pepper, pickling spice if you like it or whatever kind of spice you like. Grab an onion, peel and all, cut it in half, and throw it in. Grab a carrot, break it into 3 and throw that in there too. Break a few stalks of celery 2-3 is sufficient, throw those in and a few mashed cloves of garlic for flavor (yup I leave the skin on those too) Just mash them with a big knife! You can add fresh herbs if you like as well, or the not-so-fresh looking ones from your fridge (like parsley)

I let it simmer for 24 hours if chicken and 48 if you like for beef on the stove or in the crock pot. Alternatively, if you have an INSTANT POT you can cook for only 2.5 hours!

Now strain the ingredients, let it sit for a few minutes. Then enjoy and store extra.

HONEY MUSTARD SALAD DRESSING

- 1/4 cup dijon mustard
- 1/4 cup honey(i like raw)
- 1/4 cup apple cider vinegar (I prefer raw, unfiltered)
- 1/4 cup extra virgin olive oil
- 1 teaspoon Himalayan salt

- 1/4 teaspoon black pepper

LEMON VINAIGRETTE SALAD DRESSING

- 1/4 cup red wine vinegar
- 2 tablespoons dijon mustard
- 1/2 cup extra virgin olive oil
- Zest and juice of 1 lemon (about 4 tablespoons juice and 3 teaspoons zest)
- 1 clove garlic, finely minced OR 1 teaspoon garlic powder
- 1 tablespoon honey
- 1 teaspoon salt
- 1/4 teaspoon black pepper
- 1 tablespoon fresh minced oregano OR 2 teaspoons dried oregano

SESAME GINGER SALAD DRESSING

- 1/3 cup extra virgin olive oil
- 2 tablespoons toasted sesame oil
- 1/4 cup seasoned rice vinegar
- 1 clove garlic, finely minced OR 1 teaspoon garlic powder
- 2 tablespoons soy sauce
- 1 tablespoon honey
- 2 tablespoons peel and grated fresh ginger OR 2 teaspoons ground ginger Enjoy

Manufactured by Amazon.ca
Bolton, ON

35063263R00118